Cypriani Magici Septem Horae Magicae
Copyright © 2025 José Leitão
Translation by Brian Johnson
All Rights Reserved.

ISBN 978-1-915933-82-9 (Hardcover)
ISBN 978-1-915933-83-6 (Softcover)

A CIP catalogue for this title is available from the British Library.
10 9 8 7 6 5 4 3 2 1

Except in the case of quotations embedded in critical articles or reviews, no part of this book may be reproduced or transmitted in any form or by any means, electronic or mechanical, including photocopying, recording, or by any information storage and retrieval system, without permission in writing from the publisher. No part of this book may be used or reproduced in any manner for the purpose of training artificial intelligence technologies or systems.

José Leitão has asserted his moral right to be identified as the author of this work.

EU authorised representative:
Easy Access System Europe
Mustamäe tee 50, 10621 Tallinn, Estonia
gpsr.requests@easproject.com

Published in 2025
Hadean Press
West Yorkshire
England
https://hadean.press

UIDB/00311/2025

Cypriani Magici
Septem Horae Magicae

A study and translation of MSS. 174, n. 155
from the Portuguese National Library,
an Iberian book of pacts and treasure hunting.

Seven Magic Hours of
Cyprian the Mage

José Leitão

Contents

Introduction ... vii

Books of Saint Cyprian in the sixteenth and seventeenth centuries ... 1

Books of Saint Cyprian in the eighteenth century ... 15

Books of Saint Cyprian in the nineteenth century ... 28

The *Cypriani Magici Septem Horae Magicae* ... 46

Concluding remarks ... 66

Cypriani Magici Septem Horae Magicae Facsimile ... 68

Cypriani Magici Septem Horae Magicae Transcription ... 140

Cypriani Magici Septem Horae Magicae Translation ... 164

Appendix ... 180

Bibliography ... 215

INTRODUCTION

THE HISTORY OF the Iberian Books of Saint Cyprian is an eternally unfinished one. These are magic books, part of a certain tradition of learned magic but which seem to exist outside of learned circles; they are mentioned by name as far back as the seventeenth century but are only known in rare late eighteenth-century forms and later nineteenth-century printed editions. Between all of these steps they seem not only to shed their entire contents and acquire new elements, but also shift readership groups, social functions, and utilities. Besides their textual and material complexities, Books of Saint Cyprian also exist as purely imaginary and immaterial ideas: as the subjects of folktales and imagined repositories of fantastical power outside of human reach.[1] Yet, even with their shifting faces and bodies, these books are omnipresent titles in the worlds of Iberian and Ibero-American magic practice to this day, and a non-dismissible force and structuring element in the creation of new religious movements and, currently, the international English-speaking discourse of esoteric and magic practice.

The thorough academic mapping and understanding of these Iberian magic texts can feel like a daunting task, not only due to the historical obscurity surrounding them and the absolute scarcity of pre-contemporary examples, but also due to the academic study of such books still being a nascent field of research, where the adequate standards and historiographical methods are yet to be determined. Still, a few scholars have devoted themselves to the systematic and

---

[1] See LEITÃO - *The Immaterial Book of St. Cyprian*.

systematizing understanding of such literary expressions of culture, and some have literally gone on the road to search for unknown and undocumented manuscripts in public and private libraries, dimly lit archives or old catalogues.

Thus, for the past ten years the collective understanding of these Iberian-specific forms of written culture and literature has grown exponentially, and we currently have a respectable general idea of what these books are and have been in the past, and of how they have come to us as they are right now. However, this idea can only be said to be valid for this exact moment, based on the information scholars have managed to collect up to this instance and have shared with one another. While the historical roots of the Books of Saint Cyprian are not as obscure as they once were, the irreducible fragility of our understanding of them means that the discovery of a new manuscript, or a single inconsequential mention by an inquisitorial defendant – a word being said in a time and place where it was not supposed to have been said – can, in one instant, cast down the entire edifice of academic proposals, considerations and theories on their origin and evolution. The *Cypriani Magici Septem Horae Magicae, the Seven Magic Hours of Cyprian the Mage*, is one such manuscript: a problematic, unmovable, and undeniable data point which creates more questions than it answers.

BOOKS OF SAINT CYPRIAN IN THE SIXTEENTH AND SEVENTEENTH CENTURIES

THERE IS NO known date as to when objects with the name 'Book of Saint Cyprian' began circulating in Iberia. When it comes to date proposals, contemporary Spanish scholars seem to point to the general period of the second half of the seventeenth century as the moment when texts attributed to the fictional fourth century sorcerer turned saint, Saint Cyprian, begin to circulate in the non-Portuguese kingdoms of Iberia.² However, older chronologies, such as that by the Galician scholar Vicente Risco (1884-1963), most often place the sixteenth century as the likely origin of the Cyprian books.³ Portuguese date proposals, even if rare, tend to align themselves with Risco, placing the origin of the Books of Saint Cyprian in this kingdom in the sixteenth century, as proposed by the sociologist of religion Moisés Espírito Santo. Yet, the origin of this date by Espírito Santo is uncertain, as the only proof he offers for such a claim is that of an unidentified 'canonical Index'.⁴ This could be taken as an indication of source, but the fact that no Portuguese Index of forbidden books contains any reference to magic books attributed to Saint Cyprian places a great deal of uncertainty on such a claim.

---

2 MORALES ESTÉVES - 'Los Grimorios y Recetarios Mágicos,' p. 543.
3 RISCO - 'Los Tesoros,' p. 191.
4 ESPÍRITO SANTO - *A Religião Popular Portuguesa*, p. 125.

Beyond conjecture, what is likely the earliest document which mentions the words 'Book of Saint Cyprian' (or in this case, 'Libro de San Cipriano') is a small 1610 denunciation made with the Toledo Inquisition against the *morisco* doctor Juan de Toledo (a descendant of Iberian Muslims).[5] This date unequivocally indicates that, by the beginning of the seventeenth century, Cyprian books were already known to circulate in central Iberia and, in all likelihood, were a literary reality by the late sixteenth. Beyond the denunciation, this document does not offer much information regarding the content and structure of Juan's book, only that he used it to find treasure, having also had in his possession a *Picatrix*.[6] In this regard, it should be noted that in the Iberian seventeenth century the word 'Picatrix' can be commonly found associated with a number of astral magic texts, so this does not necessarily mean Juan had a *Picatrix* as translated from the Arabic *Ghāyat al-Ḥakīm* into Castilian and Latin in the thirteenth century.[7]

Examining Portuguese documentation, the earliest and most iconic reference to a book being referred to as a 'Book of Saint Cyprian' comes from the 1620 trial of Pedro Afonso, from the records of the Coimbra Inquisition. From what can be gathered from this lengthy document, Pedro Afonso was born around 1550, being a native and resident of the village of Fornelos, close to Vila Real. Around the year 1583 he met

---

5 CARDAILLAC-HERMOSILLA - 'Le Magicien-Guérisseur du Carnet de Voyage de 1835 d'Antoine d'Abbadie', p. 100, 107.

6 SIERRA - *Procesos en la Inquisición de Toledo*, p. 574.

7 On the *Picatrix* see SAIF - *The Arabic Influences on Early Modern Occult Philosophy*; FORSHAW - 'From Occult Ekphrasis to Magical Art'; ATTRELL and PORRECA - 'Introduction'. On the other Iberian seventeenth century 'Picatrixes' see LEITÃO - *Learned Magic in Early Modern Portugal*, p. 206-213.

Gonçalo Pais, an *almocreve* from Basto (an ambiguous location, but likely Cabeceiras de Basto).[8] The relationship between these two men is not obvious, but whatever it might have been, both ended up talking about healing and illness and it was in this context that Gonçalo claimed to own a particular book which he used to 'cure and release any person of any ills they might have', a book he claimed was of Saint Cyprian.[9]

Even though Pedro was illiterate, this Book of Saint Cyprian in Gonçalo's possession sparked his interest and, with Gonçalo's permission, Pedro took it in order to test its effectiveness. The nature of these experiments is unknown, but they were reassuring enough that Pedro paid Gonçalo 6,000 *réis* in money and olive oil in order to have it copied, a job which was performed by António Gonçalves, the priest of Celeirós.[10]

The copy being done, Pedro's Book of Saint Cyprian is mentioned as being about two fingers thick, in half-quarter.[11] Unlike Juan's Cyprian book, the content of Pedro's is described to some extent as containing several healing procedures, some more medical, others more magical. From Pedro's memory, one of these was a healing for scrofula, which he never fully describes; however, other ones, such as a cure for paralysis, are extensively discussed in his Inquisition

---

8 *Almocreve* refers to an activity in existence in Portugal until the nineteenth century, a transporter of merchandize and conductor of beasts of burden, from the Arabic *al-mukārī*.

9 'curar e despejar todas as pessoas de todos os malles que tivessem,' in ANTT, Tribunal do Santo Ofício, Inquisição de Coimbra, Processos, n°5634, fol.57r.

10 ANTT, Tribunal do Santo Ofício, Inquisição de Coimbra, Processos, n°5634, fol.57v, fol.69v.

11 'Half-quarter' is recurrently mentioned as the manuscript size. While it is impossible to confirm this, such likely makes it a half quarto, or an octavo in contemporary print sizes.

documentation.[12] This healing procedure seemed to instruct those suffering from this illness to dress themselves with their clothes either inside-out or turned backwards, being in this way accompanied by Pedro to a bridge passing over a river, where they should recite the prayer 'I am stuck and bewitched, Jesus name of Jesus, release and unbewitch me'[13] three times at the beginning of the said bridge, three times in its middle, and three times at its end. The ritual would end with three Hail Marys, after which the patient would be taken home, and there re-dress themselves with their clothes in the proper way.[14]

Another practice could be used for rifles which were found to be ineffective or mills which were not working, but it seemed to be specialized for the healing of animals and beasts of burden, such as oxen, or hunting dogs which were found to be lethargic. This was considerably more complex: the animal in question should be taken to a river where the healer should take out a sword, which should be in the shape of a cross (straight and with a perpendicular and noticeable guard), and 'cut' the stream of the river in the form of a cross three times while saying, 'I am released, in name of the Father, and the Son, and the Holy Spirit', a prayer which should be topped with three Hail Marys and

---

12 ANTT, Tribunal do Santo Oficio, Inquisição de Coimbra, Processos, n°5634, fol.57v.

13 'Eu estou pejado e emfeitiçado, Jesus nome de Jesus, despeiaime, e desenfeitiçaime', in ANTT, Tribunal do Santo Oficio, Inquisição de Coimbra, Processos, n°5634, fol.130r.

14 ANTT, Tribunal do Santo Oficio, Inquisição de Coimbra, Processos, n°5634, fol.58r.

some minor bloodlettings into the running water.[15] While this did not seem to be the prescribed method of using this particular healing, Pedro would also perform this ritual on humans, adding variations to this, such as performing it at a fountain, or, should his patient not be able to physically move to any adequate source of running water, he would perform it in their homes with a bowl of water taken from fountains which never ran dry.[16] Another ritual not mentioned by Pedro Afonso, but described by some of his clients, was one against sorcery in which he drew pentagrams on the four corners of a house with a coin or a knife, placed salt over them and recited certain unperceivable words of banishment, finally fumigating the premises with incense and herbs (artemisia being explicitly mentioned).[17]

All these cures, according to this Cyprian book, could only be used and performed on Sundays. This is not a meaningless detail as this is a frequent instruction found in the 'Prayer of Saint Cyprian',[18] a talismanic magico-religious text belonging to a wider 'Western' magico-religious arsenal, recurrently used as a method for the banishment of evil spirits, sorcery, and the evil eye, known in regions as varied as Italy, Scandinavia, and the Arabic world, and extremely

---

15 'eu me despejo, em nome do Padre, e do filho, e do espirito santo', in ANTT, Tribunal do Santo Ofício, Inquisição de Coimbra, Processos, n°5634, fol.58v, fol.60v.

16 ANTT, Tribunal do Santo Ofício, Inquisição de Coimbra, Processos, n°5634, fol.18v, 13v.

17 ANTT, Tribunal do Santo Ofício, Inquisição de Coimbra, Processos, n°5634, fol.18r-v, 12r-v.

18 ANTT, Tribunal do Santo Ofício, Inquisição de Coimbra, Processos, n°5634, fol.60v.

popular in early modern Iberia.[19] Not accidentally, the Prayer of Saint Cyprian was not only present in Pedro's book, but was likely its central element and the section which gave it its very *raison d'être*. Besides its virtues as a verbal utterance and method to banish sorcery, the evil eye, and 'bad tongues', the presence of the Prayer of Saint Cyprian in this book seemed to imbue it with talismanic properties, the same often ascribed to this prayer as a stand-alone text. Thus, should there be a difficult birth, Pedro's book should be placed over the woman's head and the words 'Jesus and Mary' said three times. Similarly, should a child not want to suckle, the book should be placed over the mother's bosom and three Apostle's Creeds and three Hail Marys recited.[20]

All these characteristics describe a book that, today, stands as largely unknown, and no copy or version of the Book of Saint Cyprian currently catalogued or identified possesses such characteristics. Overall, this seemed to be a book specializing in the healing of several ailments and the magical dispelling of negative influences, built upon the Prayer of Saint Cyprian. Not only this, but the described history of this book can be used to firmly guarantee the existence of such titles and literary traditions in Portugal as far back as the 1580s, with the Gonçalo Pais book, from which Pedro's was copied, likely being much older. Such an observation, coupled together with the Juan de Toledo denunciation, largely confirms the date proposals of both Vicente Risco and Moisés Espírito Santo (although, likely by mere chance), and the second half of the sixteenth century

---

19 DUNI - 'Esorcisti o Stregoni,' p. 273; BJÖRN GÅRDBÄCK - 'Cyprianus Förmaning,' p. 36–50; BASSET - *Les Apocryphes Éthiopiens*, p. 6-24, 38-52; PAIVA - *Bruxaria e Superstição*, p. 110, 116.

20 ANTT, Tribunal do Santo Oficio, Inquisição de Coimbra, Processos, n°5634, fol.57v-58v.

can, at this point, be set down as the earliest known record of such texts in Iberia.

Even still, the apparent joint origin of the Portuguese and Spanish Cyprian books in the late sixteenth century should not lead to considerations that these, throughout the Early Modern period, were coherent between themselves. Besides the extreme variability of purpose and apparent content observed between the Juan de Toledo and Pedro Afonso books, Marcos Antonio Lopes Veiga suggests that non-Iberian Cyprian texts were also known to enter the eastern Iberian territories by way of traveling French magicians and treasure hunters at least as early as the late-seventeenth century. This could also mean that the eventual evolution of the Spanish Cyprian books suffers from a certain degree of influence of non-Iberian magic literature upon local autochthonous texts.[21]

Moving forward, one problem which arises from the Juan de Toledo and Pedro Afonso books is that such reports are strangely isolated, particularly when we are given assurance that Pedro's book was part of a literary tradition already in existence in the late-sixteenth century. As far as the known references to Portuguese Books of Saint Cyprian go, before the eighteenth century the title 'Book of Saint Cyprian' has not been found in any other document. The Spanish case follows a similar pattern, with no further mentions of Castilian manuscripts having been so far detected, and Galicia apparently only displaying evidence of Cyprian book circulation in the late-eighteenth century.[22] Still, this apparent isolation does not mean that Pedro Afonso's book sits in a vacuum. From his descriptions it is possible to insert it into a wider cultural framework of para-learned folk culture from northern Portugal.

---

21 VEIGA - *Sob a Capa Negra*, p. 119.
22 CASTRO VICENTE - *«San Cipriano» o Mago*, p. 73.

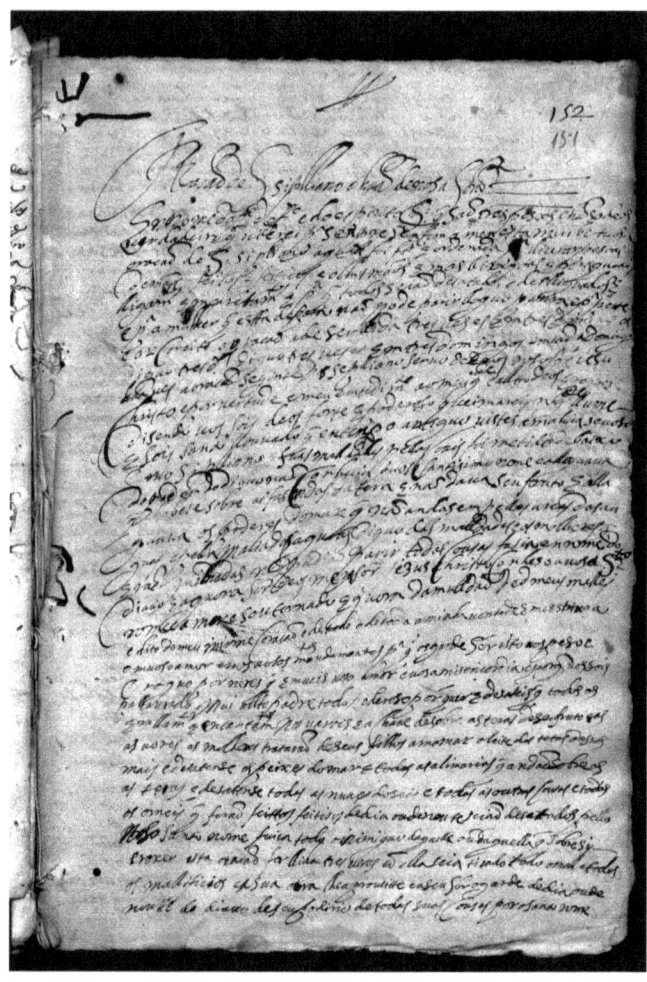

PARTIAL PRAYER OF SAINT CYPRIAN FROM THE TRIAL OF THE CARMELITE
DOMINGOS DA MADRE DE DEUS, FROM 1652.[23]

---

23 ANTT, Tribunal do Santo Ofício, Inquisição de Lisboa, Processos, n°11103, fol.151r; PT/TT/TSO-IL/028/11103, Imagem cedida pelo Arquivo Nacional da Torre do Tombo.

One particular ritual described in the Pedro Afonso book, that of taking animals or individuals to either a bridge or a riverbank and 'cutting' their illness with a sword, is attested by a number of other physicians and folk healers hailing from the Portuguese North. While not entirely similar, the 1644 trial of Maria Carvalha, from Canelas in the bishopric of Porto, mentions a similar ritual meant to 'unbind' a person, described as taking the patient 'to a bridge over a river in different evenings, making them pass through the mentioned bridge three times forward and as many [times] back, with a sword stuck between their legs, with the tip facing forward'.[24] Less than ten years later, in 1652, the trial of the Carmelite Domingos da Madre de Deus, a small-time prophet from Trofa (near Porto) at one point employed by King John IV (r.1640-1656) and who claimed communication with a familiar devil named Beltrão, equally describes such rituals.[25] In the case of Domingos, he would lead his clients to a bridge, and they would cross it from one side to the other three times while carrying a sword which had killed a man. Similar to Pedro's bloodlettings, the 'cut' illness in the Domingos ritual would be represented by a coin, which would then be dropped into the river below the bridge.[26] Other parallels between this case and that of Pedro's were that Domingos was also illiterate, but even still,

---

24 'á ponte de hum rio em differentes noutes, fazendoa passar pella dita ponte trez vezes pera diante, e outras tantas pera traz, com huã espada atravessada entre as pernas, com a ponta virada pera diante', in ANTT, Tribunal do Santo Ofício, Inquisição de Lisboa, Processos, n°7317, fol.112v.

25 See EMERSON - 'The Devil in the Court of the King'.

26 ANTT, Tribunal do Santo Ofício, Inquisição de Lisboa, Processos, n°11103, fol.74r.

frequently prescribed the Prayer of Saint Cyprian and the Prayer of Saint Leo, Pope to his clients as textual talismans.[27]

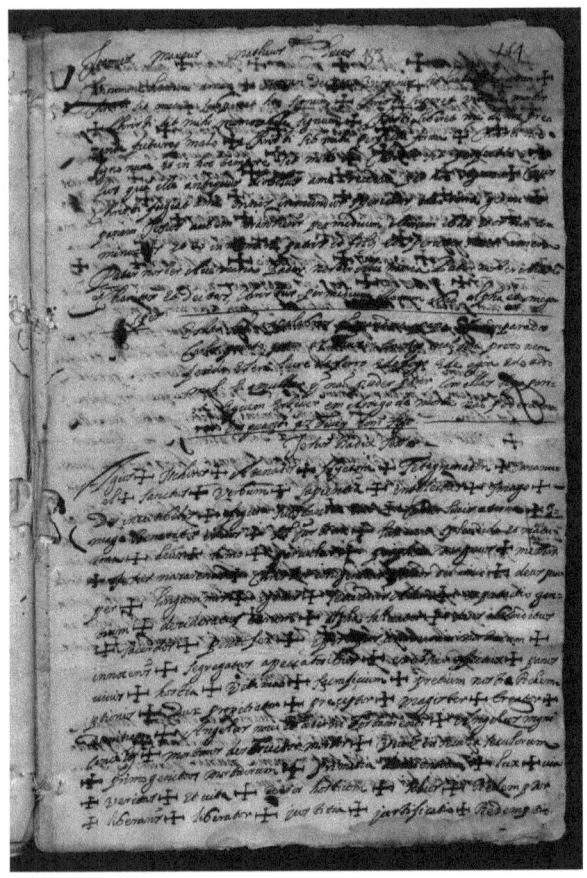

PARTIAL PRAYER OF SAINT LEO POPE, FROM THE TRIAL OF THE CARMELITE
DOMINGOS DA MADRE DE DEUS, FROM 1652.[28]

---

27 ANTT, Tribunal do Santo Ofício, Inquisição de Lisboa, Processos, n°11103, fol.69v, fol.152r-155r.

28 ANTT, Tribunal do Santo Ofício, Inquisição de Lisboa, Processos, n°11103, fol.153r; PT/TT/TSO-IL/028/11103, Imagem cedida pelo Arquivo Nacional da Torre do Tombo.

Another relevant case is that of André de Almeida, from 1656, a barber-surgeon from Bemposta (Coimbra), a committed magic practitioner known to mix folk and learned magical notions, such as using a magic dagger to draw symbols on the floor or setting up tables/altars to summon the souls in Purgatory.[29] Among the various practices in André's repertoire, his sword and bridge ritual is described as coming to a riverbank and crossing it three times while carrying a drawn sword and walking backwards (likely over a bridge).[30]

Another interesting case is that of João Vaz, a healer from Arcos, resident in Avelãs de Cima, inquired by the Inquisition in 1699 but traceable to 1680. João's story is not too different from that of Pedro Afonso, in that when one of his oxen was stricken by illness, he traveled to Óis do Bairro to see a famed healing priest named João Baptista. Baptista was apparently able to heal João's ox remotely while in his presence by reciting the Prayer of Saint Cyprian and instructing João to fumigate the animal with sulfur as soon as he got home. Having had success in this and other cases, João had this prayer eventually copied for himself into a notebook.[31] By all accounts, João's use of this Prayer of Saint Cyprian was fairly standard, in that it should only be recited on Sundays (three Sundays in a row).[32] Along with this recitation, João would occasionally mix in other procedures

---

29 ANTT, Tribunal do Santo Ofício, Inquisição de Coimbra, Processos, n°4060, fol.5r, fol.13r, fol.31r-v.

30 See PAIVA - *Bruxaria e Superstição*, p. 111; ANTT, Tribunal do Santo Ofício, Inquisição de Coimbra, Processos, n°4060, fol.22v-23r.

31 ANTT, Tribunal do Santo Ofício, Inquisição de Coimbra, Processos, n°9713, fol.8r, unnumbered.

32 ANTT, Tribunal do Santo Ofício, Inquisição de Coimbra, Processos, n°9713, unnumbered.

such as aspersions of holy water, or fumigations of sulfur.[33] João was also famed for using the Prayer of the Just Judge and another text mentioning the sons of Noah, a magic/talismanic prayer not mentioned in any Index, as well as using herbal boilings, a very common folk healing method and which he had also learned from João Baptista.[34] Not irrelevant, among the several procedures João is described as making, there are also references to the collection of water from a fountain which never ran dry, which should be gargled, spit and banished to the mar coalhado, a ritual which, in more extreme circumstances, should be done with the patient having their clothes on backwards.[35]

Similarly, in 1718, this same kind of ritual is once again found in the trial of Maria Francisca Oliveira, working in Vila Fria, here being explicitly paired with the Prayer of Saint Cyprian.[36]

---

33 ANTT, Tribunal do Santo Oficio, Inquisição de Coimbra, Processos, n°9713, fol.10r-v, unnumbered.

34 ANTT, Tribunal do Santo Oficio, Inquisição de Coimbra, Processos, n°9713, fol.11v, fol.20v, unnumbered.

35 ANTT, Tribunal do Santo Oficio, Inquisição de Coimbra, Processos, n°9713, unnumbered, Promotor, Livro n°326, fol.489r; The curdled or still sea refers to an Iberian folk magico-religious concept describing a kind of anti-world to where evil spirits and illnesses may be banished. This concept is likely derived from the tale of Saint Amaro's search for the Earthly Paradise, where the *Mar Cuajado/Coalhado* is described as being populated by sea monsters.

36 ANTT, Tribunal do Santo Oficio, Inquisição de Coimbra, Processos, n°7258, unnumbered.

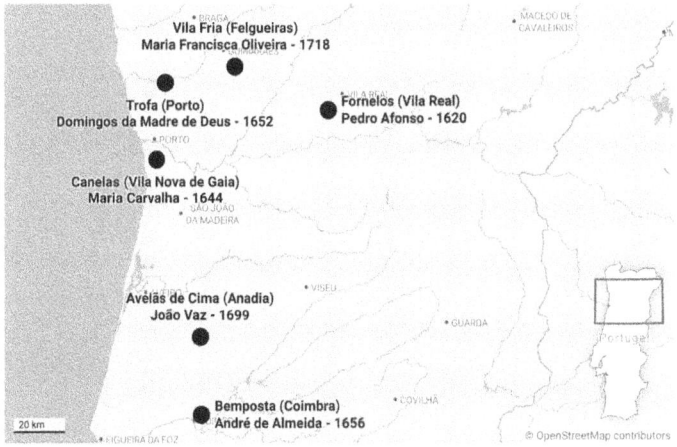

GEOGRAPHICAL LOCATIONS OF THE PEDRO AFONSO CASE AND THOSE OF
OTHER INQUISITION DEFENDANTS KNOWN TO USE HEALING METHODS SIMILAR
TO THOSE PRESENT IN HIS CYPRIAN BOOK. CREATED WITH DATAWRAPPER.

The similarities between these last five cases and the instructions contained in the Pedro Afonso book, while not providing any direct evidence of the origins or disseminations of Cyprianic literature in Portugal, seem to strongly suggest that the healings and rituals contained in the Pedro Afonso book emerged from a particular and local magic culture centered on preoccupations of healing but enacted by individuals who, while not formally educated, were not entirely without literary or financial resources. Furthermore, considerations on the Pedro Afonso case can be followed in order to establish a form of working-definition for what constituted a Book of Saint Cyprian in the Early Modern period. What the Pedro Afonso case likely indicates is that, in the sixteenth and seventeenth centuries, a Book of Saint Cyprian was simply any book of magic, be it an organized volume or a simple collection of loose and, ultimately, personal procedures, which, among its contents, contained the Prayer of Saint Cyprian. As was seen, the presence of this prayer in Pedro's book was not solely circumstantial, and it in fact imbued the book with the talismanic properties the prayer itself was believed to possess as a stand-alone text. While it cannot be claimed that this is anything more than a working-definition or an academic construction and tool of analysis, should this definition be followed, then every mention of a Prayer of Saint Cyprian one might find in any early modern Iberian document (inquisitorial or otherwise) represents a potential instance of a Book of Saint Cyprian. What ultimately distinguishes a Book of Saint Cyprian from a simple loose prayer would then be a matter of debate and analysis, being necessarily related to whether a Cyprian prayer is found isolated or grouped with other texts or ritual descriptions, or even its physical support, as either loose sheets of paper or a bound text. By this definition the João Vaz Prayer of Saint Cyprian could probably qualify as a Book of Saint Cyprian, even if this title or name is never attributed to it.

BOOKS OF SAINT CYPRIAN IN THE EIGHTEENTH CENTURY

THIS PROPOSED GENERAL understanding of an Iberian (or at least Portuguese) Book of Saint Cyprian in the seventeenth century – a book of para-learned magic emerging from folk culture, containing the Prayer of Saint Cyprian and used for healing and the banishment of evil influences – suffers a clear shift in the eighteenth century.

The research challenges of this time period are distinct from those previously mentioned. Though a superficial analysis of Portuguese inquisitorial documentation immediately notes a significant rise in mentions of Cyprian texts, the research and cataloging of these mentions is frequently marred by the internal document handling policies of the Portuguese National Archives of the Torre do Tombo, the institution responsible for the storage and preservation of the records of the Portuguese Inquisition. This signifies that, while there is a much clearer view of the evolution of the Books of Saint Cyprian in the eighteenth century, this view is still very much fragmented.

The general tendency among Cyprian books in this period seems to be the reconceptualization of these as mostly treasure hunting literature, with Saint Cyprian now emerging as the *par-excellence* patron of magic treasure hunting in Iberia – a tendency which seems to be intrinsically related to the observable rise in popularity of this style of magic in Europe at large.[37] This association of Books of Saint Cyprian

---

37 PAIVA - *Bruxaria e Superstição*, p. 160-1; DAVIES, Owen - *Grimoires*, p. 94-5.

with treasure hunting is itself not a novelty, as this was already the described use of the Juan de Toledo book in 1610; the reasoning behind this association of the Cyprian books with treasure hunting seems to once again be tied to the Prayer of Saint Cyprian. Still resting on the function of this text as a method for the banishment of evil influences, this new expression of Cyprianic literature repurposes the Cyprian prayer for the banishment of treasure-guardian spirits, often taken to be ghosts, demons, or local folkloric figures, such as *mouras encantadas*. This dichotomy surrounding the Prayer of Saint Cyprian, taken to be both a method for the banishment of evil influences and for treasure hunting, can still be seen in the contemporary nineteenth-century Portuguese *Book of Saint Cyprian*, where versions of this prayer are prescribed in different sections of this book for these two different purposes.[38] It is also relevant to note that while the majority of Cyprian book references found in the eighteenth century refer to the practice of treasure hunting, Cyprian books during this period do not become treasure hunting books exclusively. Similarly, treasure hunting books in the Portuguese territory, during this same period, are not all Cyprian books. Cyprian books and treasure hunting books are two distinct literary traditions that, in the eighteenth century, partially overlap.

Of the eighteenth-century Portuguese references to Cyprian books, the first date found is that of 1720. This is a rather fragmentary mention from the voluntary confession of Antónia Rodrigues, from Esmoriz, where it is explicitly mentioned that she owned a small notebook with the Prayer of Saint Cyprian used as protection against sorcery.[39] Shortly

---

38 ANON. - *O Grande Livro*, part 1, p. 27, 54; LEITÃO - *The Book of St. Cyprian*, p. 19, 36.

39 See ANTT, Tribunal do Santo Ofício, Inquisição de Coimbra, Processos, n°7779.

after this, in 1722-3, one finds the first instance of Saint Cyprian treasure hunting, which refers to the activities of a large group of individuals working around Guimarães. Overall, this is a pattern that will be seen on several other occasions of treasure hunting, be they related to Books of Saint Cyprian or not, with magic treasure hunting often being a group activity.[40] Macroscopically speaking, typical participants in these groups were priests, members of the low nobility, or well-to-do landowning peasants, lay collaborators potentially familiar with mines and digs and errant magic users or visionaries from various and unpredictable backgrounds, typically of a foreign origin or constituting social outsiders in some form.[41] This mix of individuals, historically observed to be overwhelmingly (but not exclusively) male, given the variety of notions and practices associated with treasure hunting, could give rise to extremely heterogeneous mixes of techniques from several socioeconomic strata and geographies.[42]

The number of individuals belonging to this 1722-3 Guimarães group is mentioned by one of its participants as being either twelve or fifteen, although only six trials have been so far found in the records of the Coimbra Inquisition, and these could only be partially examined due to the constraints mentioned above. Be that as it may, these six trials describe how a gradually increasing number of individuals began gathering to search for treasure in a place called *citânia*,

---

40 DILLINGER - *Magical Treasure Hunting in Europe and North America*, p. 163; PAIVA - *Bruxaria e Superstição*, p. 160.

41 DILLINGER - *Magical Treasure Hunting in Europe and North America*, p. 148-9, 163-4.

42 DILLINGER - *Magical Treasure Hunting in Europe and North America*, p. 162; DAVIES - *Grimoires*, p. 82; TAUSIET, María - *Urban Magic in Early Modern Spain*, p. 30-1.

a reference to a Bronze Age hillfort.[43] Central to their efforts were at least two books, one written in French and the other its translation into Portuguese, which had been produced by a man named António Fernandes. The French book seems to have been the possession of an unidentified Frenchman (the social outsider of the group), and the rituals the group engaged in seemed to be directed by a priest named Duarte Correia de Lacerda.[44] This guarantees that French influences in Iberian magic practices were not an exclusive element of the peninsula's eastern kingdoms; this same type of influence on the Portuguese side of the Cyprian books will become increasingly visible as time goes by, and particularly during the early nineteenth century.

Regarding ritual descriptions and the uses of books, there are mentions of the reading of exorcisms, the casting of rods (rabdomancy, a common feature of magical treasure hunting), and the drawing of circles and pentacles on the ground, these being surrounded by sulfur wicks, with the rods being used to flog the area around the dig.[45] As these efforts gradually proved fruitless, this group changed its strategy, and there are other reports of them attempting to summon the Devil at a crossroads on a Friday at midnight, so as to have him aid them in finding treasure. In this there are mentions of offerings being made of a single drop of Christian blood, a living kid, the foot of a goat, lamb's blood, a three-pound loaf

---

43 ANTT, Tribunal do Santo Oficio, Inquisição de Coimbra, Processos, n°8628, unnumbered.

44 ANTT, Tribunal do Santo Oficio, Inquisição de Coimbra, Processos, n°2065, fol.9r; n°7680, unnumbered; n°7692, unnumbered.

45 ANTT, Tribunal do Santo Oficio, Inquisição de Coimbra, Processos, n°8628, unnumbered.

of bread, two living roosters, and three candles. Fundamental to this ritual was the Prayer of Saint Cyprian.[46]

Following this, in 1757 one finds a denunciation from Carrazeda de Ansiães by Luís de Madureira against Mariana Lopes, which states that 'she has a book of Saint Cyprian with its rods of enchanting and disenchanting of which use I have seen, and several people and by lighting of (?) it uses a candle, walking in the night, by fountains and paths and more, [she] usually passes and enters into houses where there are people, and during the day without anyone seeing [her], and in the night with the light lit, she does the same, which has happened to me the denouncer'.[47] While extremely fragmented, this instance seems to indicate a Cyprian book both used for rabdomancy (likely related to treasure hunting) and containing instructions for the creation of something akin to a *main de gloire*, a magic candle made from a dead man's hand purported to be able to paralyze individuals or make its user imperceptible when entering a house.[48]

The very following year, another fragmented denunciation by Domingos Lopes Nogueira accused Isabel de Morais, from the town of Vinhais, of 'curing and discovering treasure, and wanting to discover stolen things, saying to these rustic people

---

46 ANTT, Tribunal do Santo Oficio, Inquisição de Coimbra, Processos, n°7689, unnumbered; n°7680, unnumbered; n°2065, unnumbered.

47 'ella tem hum livro de São Sepriano com suas varas de encantar e desencantar das cais tenho visto usar, e varias pessoas e acender do (?) delles usar hua vela andado de noite por fontes e caminhos e mais que costuma passar e entrai em casas aonde há gente e de dia sem ninguem over e de noute ainda com luz aceza, faz o mesmo, o que tém sucedido de mim denunciante', in ANTT, Tribunal do Santo Oficio, Inquisição de Coimbra, Promotor, Livro n°392, fol.434r.

48 DAVIES, Owen - *Grimoires*, p. 100.

that for all these things she resorted to a book of Saint Cyprian and that without this she could not do anything, and that she could make the poor wealthy'.[49] Further details offered by Domingos Nogueira do clarify that Isabel's book was, in fact, a fraud, being merely a book by Virgil she could flash at her clients as a tool of authority.

In 1788, one finds the trial of the Braga scrivener Diogo José Barbosa, where he, besides admitting to forging medical licenses, also confesses to having copied a book owned by an individual either named Manuel António Pereira or Julião Ribeiro.[50] This book, by Diogo's recollection, was 'written by hand, written in the Portuguese language and already very old and very used, which spoke greatly about treasure, and which also had some painted figures, in black ink, which he the Defendant also copied, and everything in the same way, as was in there, and he does not remember nor did he investigate what these meant, he solely assumes everything was meant to discover treasures'.[51] This book, being apprehended by the Inquisition, and examined by Diogo in one of his sessions, is

---

49 'fazer curas, a descobrir thezouros, e a querer descobrir couzas furtadas dizendo a esta gente rustica que para tudo isto lhe valia hum livro de São Cyprião e que sem elle não podia fazer couza alguma, e que podia fazer aos pobres ricos', in ANTT, Tribunal do Santo Ofício, Inquisição de Coimbra, Promotor, Livro n°394, fol.207r.

50 ANTT, Tribunal do Santo Ofício, Inquisição de Coimbra, Processos, n°8183, fol.4v, fol.17r.

51 'escripto em letra de mão, escripto na lingoa Portuguesa e já velho e muito curado, que falava muyto em tezouros e que tinha tambem humas feguras pintadas de tinta preta, que elle reo tambem copiou, tudo do mesmo modo que ali estavão, e senão lembra nem indagou o que se segnificavão somente julga que tudo se dirigia para se descobrirem tezouros', in ANTT, Tribunal do Santo Oficio, Inquisição de Coimbra, Processos, n°8183, fol.4v-5r.

further described as 'a manuscript bound in a folder in quarter, and which begins [with] : Spirit : and further down, inside a circle : the man with the discalced feet : and it finishes [with] : of Saint Cyprian Martyr : with this same book having almost half of its pages blank'.[52] Further descriptions mention it contained 'vain, superstitious and sortilegous things attributed to Saint Cyprian, for the purposes of disenchanting treasures by means of circles, ceremonies, imprecations, and prayers of erroneous and absurd words mixed with holy ones, and crosses, water, blessed candles, and said by a priest, dressed in an alb and stole'.[53]

According to what can be understood from the Diogo Barbosa trial, this book was not destroyed; but rather added to the (relapse) trial documentation of Manuel António.[54] This trial record has not been located, though there is also the possibility that this Cyprian book was stored in a *Caderno do Promotor* (Prosecutor's Notebook) – large collections of documents produced by the Inquisition which did not lead to formal trials. Efforts to consult these at the Portuguese National Archives have so far been fruitless.

---

52 'manuscripto encadernado em pasta em quarto, e que principa : Espirito : e mais abaixo dentro de hum circulo : o homem com os pes descalços : e acaba : de S. Cipriano Martiri : ficando o mesmo livro com quasi metade das folhas em branco,' in ANTT, Tribunal do Santo Ofício, Inquisição de Coimbra, Processos, n°8183, fol.9v.

53 'couzas vans, supersticiozas e sortilegas atribuidas a S. Cypriano, para o fim de dezencantar tizoiros por meio de circulos, ceremonias, imprecaçoens e oraçoens de palavras erroneas e absurdas misturadas com outras santas, e cruzes, agua, velas bentas ditas por hum sacerdote revestido de alva e estolla', in ANTT, Tribunal do Santo Ofício, Inquisição de Coimbra, Processos, n°8183, fol.17r.

54 ANTT, Tribunal do Santo Ofício, Inquisição de Coimbra, Processos, n°8183, fol.17r.

Approaching the end of the century, in 1790 a series of trials were initiated against another large group of individuals for events happening around September or October of 1788. These were mentioned as having taken place around Póvoa do Varzim, in a place called *cividade do Terroso*, a known and currently well researched hillfort. This treasure dig was initiated by a scrivener from Barcelos by the name of Jerónimo António, who had somehow acquired 'a book that carried the manuscript exorcisms of Saint Cyprian, and thus they called it' in Porto, and Manuel Joaquim de Faria Vilas Boas, a landowner with apparent rights over a part of Terroso.[55] Gradually these two men managed to gather a significant number of individuals from Barcelos, around ten by some counts, among whom were Manuel's priest brother António de Faria Vilas Boas and another priest by name Jerónimo Ribeiro Pais de Faria.[56]

Eventually all of them traveled to Terroso, where they flattened a large parcel of land with hoes and drew a circle and a pentagram on this land with a sword, further drawing a cross in the center of these.[57] Inside the circles they lit some candles, and placed five horseshoes taken from a black mule and some herbs.[58] This being done, all those involved gathered inside the circle, by which time the priest Jerónimo,

---

55 'hum livro que levava manuscripto, os exorcismos de S. Cypriano, que assim lhe chamavaõ,' in ANTT, Tribunal do Santo Oficio, Inquisição de Coimbra, Processos n°732, fol.4r; n°723, fol.7v, fol.13r-v

56 ANTT, Tribunal do Santo Oficio, Inquisição de Coimbra, Processos, n°732, fol.3v.

57 ANTT, Tribunal do Santo Oficio, Inquisição de Coimbra, Processos, n°730, fol.4r.

58 ANTT, Tribunal do Santo Oficio, Inquisição de Coimbra, Processos, n°727, fol.4r.

in a surplice and a stole, read the 'Exorcisms of Saint Cyprian' from a manuscript book written in Latin, while a black chicken was set loose in the circle. After a while all were ordered to kneel and the Penitential Psalms were read as holy water was spread around the area. Finally, in an unusual step, one of the members of the group, who had brought a wether (a castrated male sheep), picked this animal up and walked around the circle three times. From the remaining description, after waiting for about an hour and a half for some sort of event to happen, the group was discouraged and gradually abandoned the location.[59]

Finally, closing off the eighteenth century, another fragmentary denunciation from Alijó in 1800, made by a certain Francisco Pinto de Azevedo and João Pinto da Veiga, mentions that, while out in the fields one evening they heard the voice of the priest José de Barros Falcão saying that, 'much money would come out and the same placed his surplice and stole and struck a new fire and lit two candles and they placed them inside two lamps and [he] sat in the middle and casting holy water took a rod and made a circle and hit the floor once to the north and another to the south, and opening a missal he was reading and afterwards took a book of gospels and also read some and then took another book and was also reading from this, as we heard of Saint

---

59 ANTT, Tribunal do Santo Oficio, Inquisição de Coimbra, Processos, n°732, fol.4r; n°5197, unnumbered.

Cyprian we were afraid and ran'.[60]

While all such mentions of treasure hunting and Cyprian book appear to be rather heterogeneous and distinct, there are some common threads among the rituals mentioned. It is likely that all such manuscripts in circulation during this century did organize themselves along a small number of genealogical lines, by which methodological patterns could be established; however, what also likely happened was that those involved in such rituals and practices would add personal variations and compromises to each ritual enactment.

GEOGRAPHICAL LOCATIONS OF THE KNOWN EIGHTEENTH-CENTURY PORTUGUESE INQUISITION MENTIONS OF BOOKS OF SAINT CYPRIAN. CREATED WITH DATAWRAPPER.

---

60 'ade sair munto dinheiro e o mesmo botou sobrepelis e estola e ferio lume novo e asendeu duas velas e as meteram dentro de duas allinternas e se sentou no meio e lançando agua benta pegou em huma vara e fez hum circulo e deu huma pancada para o Norte e outra para o Sul e abrindo hum misal esteve lendo e depois pegou em hum livro de avangelios tambem leu huns poucos e depois pegou em outro livro e tambem esteve lendo como ouvimos falar em S. Sepriam tivemos medo e fogymos', in ANTT, Tribunal do Santo Oficio, Inquisição de Coimbra, Promotor, Livro n°416, fol.269r.

Besides these considerable mentions, it should be noted that all known pre-contemporary Cyprian manuscripts belong to this style of treasure hunting Book of Saint Cyprian, and they, so far, number only two. One of these can be currently found in the Reserved and Special Collections of the General Library of the University of Coimbra, referred to as MS. 2559, and having, at some point in the past, been given the title *Orações Várias para Afugentar o Demonio*; or *Various Prayers to Drive Away the Devil*. Contrary to what this title might suggest, this book does not constitute a collection of prayers; rather, it contains one single and lengthy ritual meant for the disenchantment of treasure, which bases itself on the repeated recitation of the Prayer of Saint Cyprian. While this text is written in the vernacular, it is clearly meant for priestly use, with mentions of the recitation of psalms and litanies. This manuscript has already gone through extensive analyses, being currently published in two different editions and largely accessible to an international readership.[61] The second of these manuscripts is a relatively new discovery by the researcher Félix Castro Vicente and currently rests in private hands. While it is not my place to discuss this book to a significant extent, the little which is currently known of this manuscript marks it as considerably distinct from MS. 2559, being, first of all, entirely written in Latin and containing several magic circle designs.

---

61 See, LEITÃO - *Opuscula Cypriani*, p. 117-257 and LEITÃO - *The Coimbra Book of Saint Cyprian*.

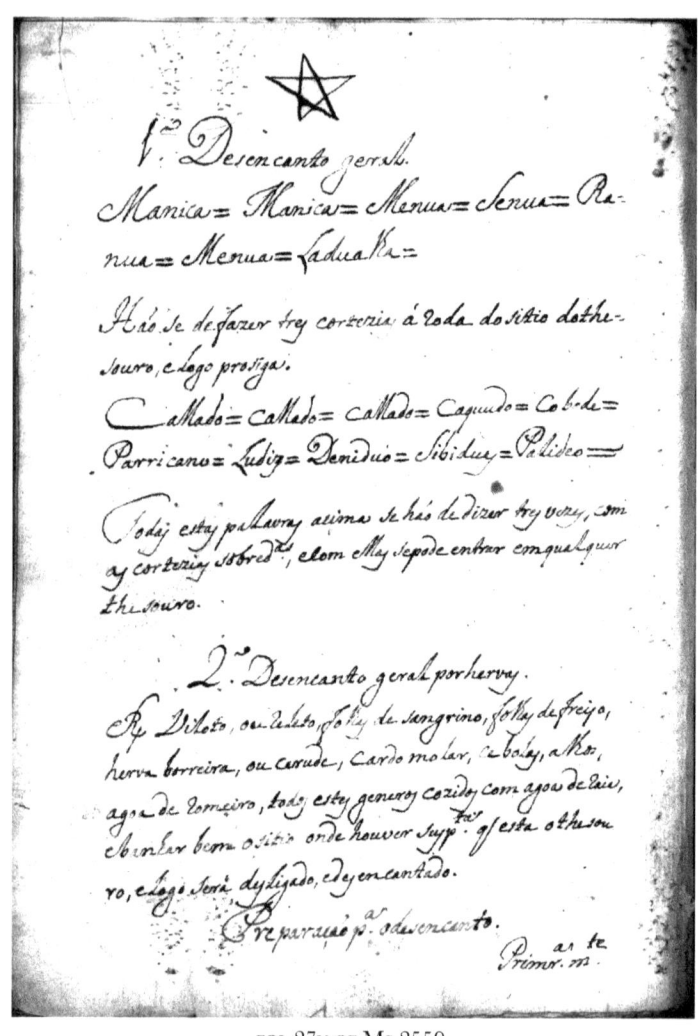

fol.27v of Ms.2559,
[Orações Várias para Afugentar o Demonio].[62]

---

62 BGUC, Reservados, [Orações Várias para Afugentar o Demonio], n.d., Ms.2559, fol.27v-28r; images provided by the General Library of the University of Coimbra.

Primr.[te] m.[to] Se leva agoa benta, e se lança sobre o sitio, e a o ador delle = Todos dirão o acto decontrição, e a Ladainha de N. Snr., pedindo lhe auxilio, e ajuda, e tambem o Psalmo Miserere mei Deus, athé o verso Tibi soli peccavi, e alguny mais pedindo a D. misericordia = Logo concorra com o seu juros coração, e com os conjuros deS. Cypriano = Depois farão hũ circulo bem longo á roda de todo o sitio p.[a] cavar dentro nelle = Logo se conjurarão os demonios com pena de obed.[a] p.[a] o Lugar q[ue] lhes for nomeado, p.[a] q[ue] não impeção o tirar aquelle haver, nem o mudem, nem o affundem, e o conservem na m.[ma] especie em q[ue] se pos, sem traz mutação, ou diminuição, nem separação p.[r] p.[e] alguma, com pena de obed.[a] do P.[e] Filho, e Esp.[to] S.[to]

Prosegue se com o Psalmos, e o conjuro em q[ue] se tira, até rado q[ue] seja, conjura se p.[a] q[ue] o demonio não tenha mais poder naquelle haver, Lançando lhe agoa benta, Lavando nella o q[ue] se achar: exorcigmará Logo o Lugar p.[a] q[ue] o demonio se afugente delle, e não torne mais; e caso q[ue] pareção alguãs visoens, conjura lhas, pondo lhys preceito, q[ue] não impeção, ou inquietem o tirar aquelle haver, Lançando lhe agoa benta = Se houver fantasma, bicho, ou outro qual quer animal, não ha q[ue] temer: Ment[e] se e
                           Conjura se

FOL.28R OF MS.2559,
[ORAÇÕES VÁRIAS PARA AFUGENTAR O DEMONIO].

BOOKS OF SAINT CYPRIAN IN THE NINETEENTH CENTURY

THE NINETEENTH CENTURY largely spells the final crystallization of the various forms and streams of content which characterized the Books of Saint Cyprian during the previous three hundred years as they become printed commodities. Still, before that, the Portuguese Inquisition, which would only be extinguished in 1821, would produce one more report. This was the 1802 case of the priest Rafael Lopes Ramos Fonseca.

Rafael was a member of the secular clergy in Braga, famed as an exorcist. While this was not a problem in itself, the issue in his trial was that he, at some point, had picked up a number of illicit practices and a Book of Saint Cyprian, all of which were coloring an otherwise licit activity as superstitious or plainly magical. Among the several reports of Rafael's activities lies one where he was called to heal a woman, and after investigating the case, he determined that the illness affecting his client was caused by a buried treasure hiding in her basement. Thus, his Book of Saint Cyprian was brought into play in order to enact a magic treasure dig and banish the harmful treasure guardian present. Not much is mentioned regarding this book, as the Inquisition's main preoccupation with Rafael was the issue of his unlicensed exorcisms, but this is still described as a manuscript book, and that this ritual required the removal of all Christian elements from its vicinity and the burning of specific herbs. There are also mentions of the use of coscinomancy (divination with a sieve), although it is uncertain if the instructions for this were present in Rafael's manuscript.[63]

Otherwise, by the mid-nineteenth century, what could today be called the 'standard' Portuguese and Spanish versions of the *Book of Saint Cyprian* begin appearing in commercial bookstores. Both versions are distinct and each of them emerges from particular publishing contexts, yet both possess ample similarities and seem to distinguish themselves through an unclear process of divergent evolution. As such, how the current Portuguese and Spanish versions of the Cyprian book came to be what they are is still a story unto itself, and one which, like all others referring to these books, is not fully understood. Out of both main versions, the current Portuguese one seems to have the more linear evolution.

It is known that several different versions of the *Book of Saint Cyprian* were produced during the nineteenth century, with several of these being only known through secondhand quotes and references by occasional ethnographers and folklorists (such as Francisco' Adolfo Coelho, who shall be amply discussed below).[64] However, among all of them, one version seems to establish itself as a major trend-setter among the subsequent Portuguese editions: *O Verdadeiro e Ultimo Livro de S. Cypriano*, or *The True and Last Book of St. Cyprian*. This was a two-part book, already possessing in itself much of the content of the current 'standard' Portuguese book, and carrying indelible marks from the history of this form of literature from the past three centuries, such as uses of the Prayer of Saint Cyprian for the banishment of evil spirts (using some of the particular nomenclature already present

---

63 ANTT, Tribunal do Santo Oficio, Inquisição de Coimbra, Processos, n°9846, unnumbered.

64 COELHO - 'Notas e Parallelos Folkloricos I, p. 171-2; COELHO - *Obra Etnográfica*, vol. 2, p. 228-9.

in the Rafael 1802 manuscript, like the notion of an open or closed body) and the finding of treasure. Besides this, *The True and Last Book* also included sections clearly derived from erudite textual sources.

In time this book generated two offshoots, one being a small book, entitled *Verdadeiro Livro de S. Cypriano ou Thesouro Particular do Feiticeiro*,[65] the *True Book of St. Cyprian or the Sorcerer's Private Treasure*, containing reduced forms of some of the rituals present in *The True and Last Book*, and which all known editions and references place as a Porto-specific product, or a Porto Book. The other offshoot of *The True and Last Book* was a larger work, *O Grande Livro de S. Cypriano ou Thesouro do Feiticeiro*,[66] *The Great Book of St. Cyprian or the Sorcerer's Treasure*, which contained the entire contents of *The True and Last Book* but also added a third part to it, and which is consistently found printed in Lisbon, a Lisbon Book. By whatever commercial or market laws, in time the Porto Book seems to disappear from print and the Lisbon Book becomes the dominant version of this textual tradition and what today one might consider the 'standard' Portuguese version. Besides this, *The Great Book of St. Cyprian*, being transported to Brazil by the end of the nineteenth century and throughout the twentieth, became the source of other offshoots and versions of this literary tradition across the Atlantic.

---

[65] An English translation of this book can be consulted in LEITÃO - *Opuscula Cypriani*, p. 318-350

[66] An English translation of this book is currently published by Hadean Press, see LEITÃO - *The Book of St. Cyprian*.

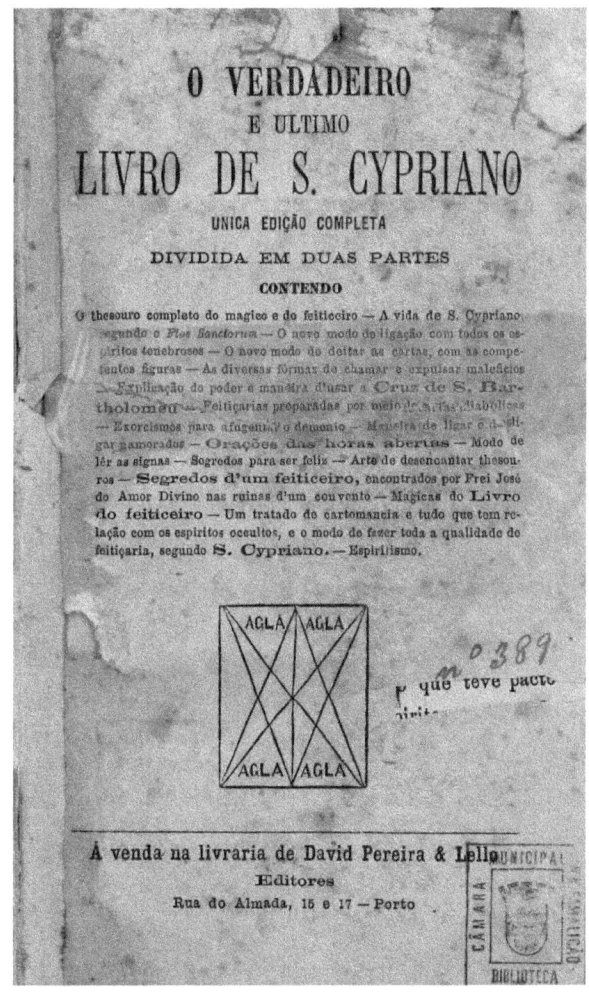

Cover of the Portuguese *O Verdadeiro e Ultimo Livro de S. Cypriano*, the two-part book.[67]

---

67 Image provided by the Biblioteca Municipal Camilo Castelo Branco (Vila Nova de Famalicão), Sala de Fundo Local, BMCCB-FL VC 133 VERD.

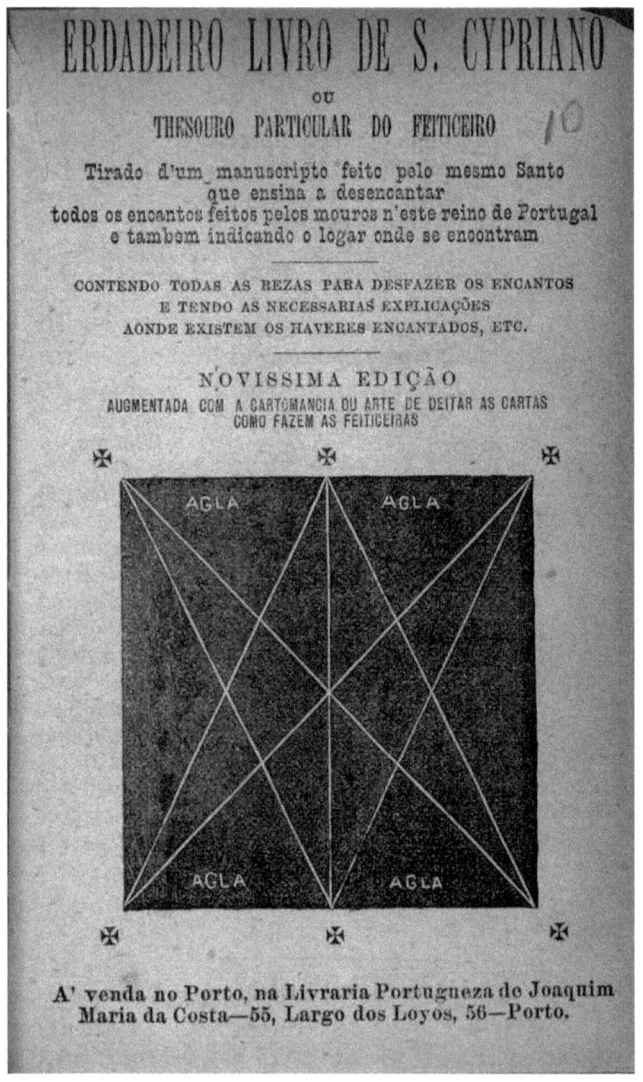

Cover of the Portuguese *Verdadeiro Livro de S. Cypriano*, the reduced Porto book.

COVER OF THE PORTUGUESE *O GRANDE LIVRO DE S. CYPRIANO*, THE THREE-PART LISBON BOOK.

The Spanish side of the matter is likely more complicated. While the 'standard' Cyprian book in that country can be given several different titles with each having slight variations in content, it is a text usually attributed to the German monk Jonas Sufurino.[68] This book is not radically separated from the current 'standard' Portuguese version, and both share a number of points. As a major distinguishing factor, the Sufurino Book contains a much greater amount of material identifiable with non-Iberian sources, such as the *Black Pullet*, but most relevantly the *Grand Grimoire*, a French and Italian mid-eighteenth century derivative from Solomonic literature.[69] Even so, the Sufurino Book also possesses a method for the banishment of evil spirits which appears to be a reduced version of that present in both the Portuguese two-part *True and Last Book* and the three-part Lisbon Book, possibly indicating one of these as its precursor.[70] However, when it comes to one of the fundamental aspects of the Cyprian literary tradition – that of treasure hunting –, the Sufurino Book seems to disregard the Prayer of Saint Cyprian, instead addressing it through the magic methodologies of the *Grand Grimoire*. Furthermore, this is not the only treasure hunting section in this book, and it also contains instructions for the production of a magic candle made with human fat whose flame will point in the direction of buried treasure and which once again forgoes the use of the Prayer of Saint

---

68 See for example ANON. - *Libro de San Cipriano*. An English translation of this book is currently published by Nephilim Press, see MAGGI - *Sufurino*. For a partial overview of the several Spanish (and some of the Portuguese) printed *Books of Saint Cyprian* see CASTRO VICENTE - 'El Libro de San Cipriano (I)' and CASTRO VICENTE - 'El Libro de San Cipriano (y II)'.
69 DAVIES - *Grimoires*, p. 101.
70 ANON. - *Libro de San Cipriano*, p. 85.

Cyprian.[71] This same Sufurino Book is also frequently at the base of several other editions, such as the *Libro Infernal*, a lengthy book containing material from the *Grand* and *Petite Albert* and the *Key of Solomon*, or the *La Magia Suprema Negra, Roja e Infernal de los Caldeos y de los Egipcios*, a self-styled sequel to the Sufurino Book.[72]

Standing outside of this line are other known Spanish books, such as the *Heptameron ó Elementos Magicos Compuesto por el Gran Cipriano*, *Heptameron or Magic Elements Composed by the Great Cyprian*, a distinct work from the *Heptameron* attributed to Pietro d'Abano. Also, side by side with such titles, and constantly crosspollinating them during the boom of Spanish Saint Cyprian publications, stand a significant number of Spanish versions of the *Grand Grimoire*, such as the *Secretos del Infierno*, or the *Secrets of Hell* (with a known publication date at least as early as 1835).[73] Furthermore, in 1885, the Galician journalist, historian, and poet Bernardo Barreiro, in his *Brujos y Astrólogos de la Inquisicion de Galicia*, purports to publish a *Book of Saint Cyprian* as a kind of appendix to this work, but in doing so rather presents a *Grand Grimoire*, indicating some sort of equivalence between these two titles in various Spanish regions.[74]

---

71 ANON. - *Libro de San Cipriano*, p. 135.

72 An English translation of this book is currently published by Hadean Press; see SUFURINO and SAVEDOW (trans.) - *The Supreme Black, Red and Infernal Magic of the Chaldeans and Egyptians*.

73 My heartfelt acknowledgement to Félix Castro Vicente for having provided me with several versions of this title.

74 BARREIRO - *Brujos y Astrólogos de la Inquisición de Galicia*, p. 126-149.

COVER OF THE SPANISH *LIBRO DE SAN CIPRIANO*, THE SUFURINO BOOK.

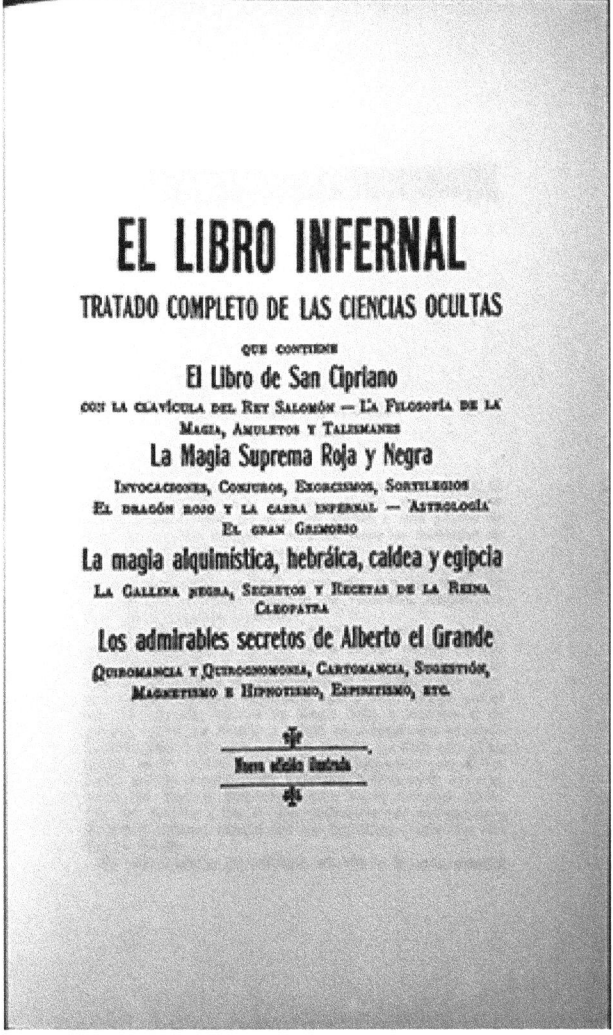

COVER OF THE EXTENSIVE SPANISH *LIBRO INFERNAL*.

Cover of the Spanish *La Magia Suprema Negra, Roja e Infernal de los Caldeos y de los Egipcios*, a self-styled sequel to the Sufurino book.

COVER OF THE SPANISH CYPRIANIC *HEPTAMERON Ó ELEMENTOS MAGICOS*.

While the influence of the *Grand Grimoire* in Iberian Saint Cyprian literature is most visible in Spain, it should be noted that there are known cases of early *Grand Grimoire* material crosspollination with Portuguese Cyprian texts and practices. While only one pre-nineteenth century instance of this has so far been detected, its early date marks it as a fundamental piece in understanding the circulation and conception of magic treasure hunting literature in Iberia, be it attributed to Saint Cyprian or not.

A previously unmentioned treasure hunting Inquisition case, from 1784, describes how a large treasure hunting party was active in the border region of Freixo de Espada à Cinta up to Bragança.[75] This group was fairly well-known in the region, and it involved individuals from not only Freixo de Espada à Cinta proper, but also Mós, Lagoaça, Carviçais, Torre de Moncorvo, and Mogadouro. This group was also known to cross the border into Castile to hunt treasure, having contacts with other such treasure hunters around the Salamanca region. Whatever their exact practices, this group is noted as having very little success in its efforts, and in order to attempt to change their fortunes, a number of them eventually contacted a poor carpenter named António Redondo, a native of Mós residing in Carviçais. From their initial approach these individuals seemed to simply want António to join their group, telling him tales that 'if they had a *Book of Saint Cyprian* and a cleric to make the banishments to the enchanters of the treasure, they would easily get them'.[76] Having captured António's attention,

---

[75] ANTT, Tribunal do Santo Ofício, Inquisição de Coimbra, Processos, n°3951, unnumbered.

[76] 'se ouvesse hum livro de S. Supriano e hum clerigo que fizeça esconjuros aos encantadores dos tizouros facilmente os conseguiriam,' in ANTT, Tribunal do Santo Ofício, Inquisição de Coimbra, Processos, n°3951, unnumbered.

he joined their group a few days later as they went to dig in a nearby hillfort, referred to as *Castelo de Torronho*, in Carviçais. On this occasion the group had with them a foreigner named either Vicente Morigani or Murigune, a silversmith living in Murça (Vila Real) who was also famed as a *vedor* (a seer), a term frequently used to refer to someone believed to be able to see inside both the earth and human bodies.[77]

The group attempted a few digs with no success, and this was when the topic of the *Book of Saint Cyprian* was brought up again, and that for them to more easily find treasure, someone in the group should volunteer to perform a pact. It was at this time that the reason behind António's invitation to join the group was revealed, and he was hard-pressed to make this pact, which he acceded to.[78] While this is an unusual situation, such tactics are not unheard of in the wider worlds of Portuguese treasure hunting and Saint Cyprian practices. Particularly, in a folktale from Vinhais, one of the many which feature the *Book of Saint Cyprian* as a fundamental narrative device, it is mentioned that a group convinced a poor Galician man to offer his soul to the Devil in order for them to find treasure.[79] Despite this folktale reference, it should be noted that the issue of diabolical pacts associated with the *Book of Saint Cyprian* is otherwise rare, but this point is immediately clarified by the description of the pact ritual offered by Vicente Morigani, which, in every detail, mimics that present in the *Grand Grimoire*: 'making a triangle with a bloodstone on the location of the treasure, being inside this and having in his hand a hazel rod and

---

77 ANTT, Tribunal do Santo Ofício, Inquisição de Coimbra, Processos, n°3951, unnumbered; n°3949, unnumbered.

78 ANTT, Tribunal do Santo Ofício, Inquisição de Coimbra, Processos, n°3951, unnumbered.

79 LEITÃO - *The Immaterial Book of St. Cyprian*, p. 74-5.

saying these formal words: oh Lucifugi Astoti prince of all spirits, should thou not favor me in this quest with the largest and closest treasure I shall punish thee with the great words of the Clavicula: and hitting the ground with the rod would the treasure be unearthed and cast out of the earth'.[80]

Agreeing to the deal, the whole group gathered a few days later to go on an expedition to Castile, crossing the border in two different groups and gathering in Vitigudino. From there they traveled to Tamames, where they met a messenger from a Castilian treasure hunting group. They stayed in that location for some time, though Vicente and one other member of the group traveled northeast to Salamanca in order acquire some of the necessary magic implements and also to have the *Book of Saint Cyprian* in their possession translated, as this was apparently in French.[81] All of this creates a great deal of uncertainty when it comes to the accurate understanding and interpretation of the book this group carried. It should be noted that this is always addressed as a *Book of Saint Cyprian*, but not only is its known content coincidental with the *Grand Grimoire*, it also seems to be a non-local text. Furthermore, this book was printed, not a manuscript.[82]

---

80 'feito hum triangulo com huma pedra matildes no lugar do tizouro, metido dentro tendo na mão huma vara de aveleira se deziam estas formaes palavras: ó lucifugi astoti pricipe de todos os esperitos se não me favoreças nesta demanda com o tizouro mais grande e mais proximo eu te castigarei com as grandes palavras de clavicula: e batendo com a vara no cham se dezentranhava o tizouro e saia para fora da terra,' in ANTT, Tribunal do Santo Oficio, Inquisição de Coimbra, Processos, n°3951, unnumbered.

81 SILVA - *Nova Configuração da Inquisição Portuguesa em Meio a Iluminados e Iluministas*, p. 321; ANTT, Tribunal do Santo Oficio, Inquisição de Coimbra, Processos, n°3949, unnumbered.

82 ANTT, Tribunal do Santo Oficio, Inquisição de Coimbra, Processos, n°3951, unnumbered.

There are various possible resolutions for the identification of this book. The first and most obvious was that this was, indeed, an eighteenth-century French printed *Grand Grimoire*, which was transported to Portugal by the mentioned Vicente (who was likely Italian) and, it being a book dealing with treasure hunting, was (mis)identified by the locals as a Book of Saint Cyprian. Alternately, even if this was a French printed book, and even if its content was the same as a *Grand Grimoire*, it is also possible that its association with Saint Cyprian was inherent to itself, as France is known to have its own Cyprianic literary lines. But be that as it may, this case guarantees the presence of the *Grand Grimoire*, or *Grand Grimoire*-related texts in late eighteenth-century Portugal, with the interactions between this and the local Cyprian tradition becoming increasingly felt in the early nineteenth century before disappearing from the 'standard' genealogy of the Portuguese Porto and Lisbon Books.

As the case progressed, the Salamanca party returned with a bloodstone and some parchment, and the whole group traveled south to El Cabaco, where they were joined by seven or eight Castilians, among whom were a priest and a sacristan who were carrying holy water, candle holders, and the remaining necessary magic tools. As the group settled, António, Vicente, and a few other members went to an abandoned house to perform the pact and summon the spirit 'Lucifugi'. The plan seems to have been for António to indeed perform the pact, but as soon as Lucifugi manifested and brought forth a buried treasure, the priest would leap into action and, with holy water and exorcisms, banish him and dissolve the pact. Either way, 'the same Vicente made a triangle on the ground with a bloodstone and placed in the middle of this two candle holders with lit candles, and all the remaining [individuals] removing themselves, ordered him the Defendant to enter the triangle, having in his hand a hazel rod which he the Defendant had cut the previous day at the rising of the sun with a virgin knife, or which had not cut any other circumstantial thing, which were thus needed and prescribed in the book, which was printed'.[83] A sheet of parchment with a written pact was taken out and the words 'I make this writing of delivery of my soul to the Devil, should he give me this treasure' were spoken, but nothing happened.[84]

Disappointment over the failure of the ritual spread quickly, and that very day the large group began to break apart, with the Portuguese members making their way back, though they stopped in Aldeiadávila. Once there, the group went to a place called Fonte da Menda, where the ritual was tried once again and where it once again produced no results. Shortly after, António and a few of his companions returned home, but some stayed in Castile, where they became counterfeiters.[85]

Going back into the mid-nineteenth-century printed Books of Saint Cyprian, their origin and emergence out of the previously attested manuscript culture is not obvious.

---

83 'o mesmo Vicente fez no cham hum triangolo com huma pedra matildes e pôs no meio os dois castiçaes com as vellas acezas e retirandose os mais o mandou a elle Reo meter no triangollo tendo na mão huma vara de aveleira que elle mesmo Reo no dia antecedente ao nascer do sol tinha cortado com huma navalha virgem ou que não tinha cortado outra couza cincunstanveis que eram percizas e prescrevia o livro que era impresso,' in ANTT, Tribunal do Santo Ofício, Inquisição de Coimbra, Processos, n°3951, unnumbered.

84 'Eu faço este escrito de entregar a minha alma ao Demonio se me der este tizouro,' in ANTT, Tribunal do Santo Ofício, Inquisição de Coimbra, Processos, n°3951, unnumbered.

85 ANTT, Tribunal do Santo Oficio, Inquisição de Coimbra, Processos, n°3951, unnumbered.

We can detect clear instances of general thematic and methodological continuities, and we can equally detect the introduction of novel non-Iberian content into this literary stream. The late eighteenth and early nineteenth centuries, when all these new models, arrangements, and negotiations between magic and literary traditions took place, is thus an obscure period in the history of the Iberian Cyprian books.

It is here that the *Cypriani Magici Septem Horae Magicae* fits, right in the middle point between the transition from manuscript to print, between folk and learned, and between Iberia and Europe.

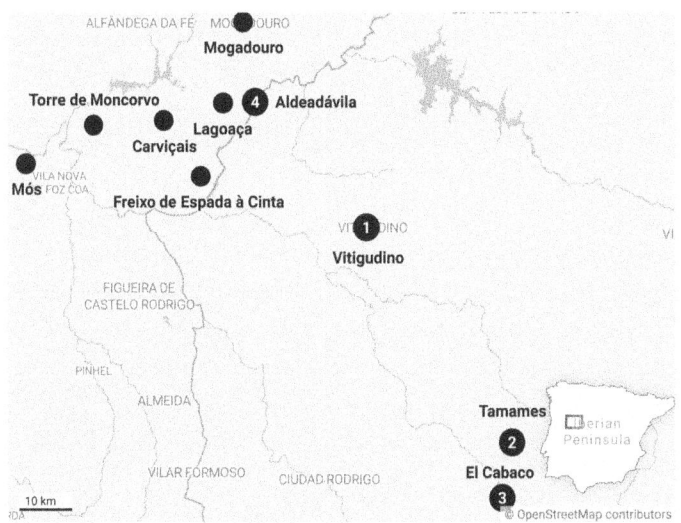

ORIGINS AND KNOWN TRAVELS OF THE *BOOK OF SAINT CYPRIAN/GRAND GRIMOIRE* TREASURE HUNTING PARTY OF ANTÓNIO REDONDO. CREATED WITH DATAWRAPPER.

THE CYPRIANI MAGICI SEPTEM HORAE MAGICAE

THE ONLY KNOWN copy of the *Cypriani Magici Septem Horae Magicae* has a history of its own. Its date of production is, at this point, unknown, as is its author and region of origin. The earliest reference we have to it is an 1888 article by the philologist, ethnographer, and pedagogue Francisco Adolfo Coelho (1847-1919). This was published in the very first issue of the *Revista Lusitana*, an historical publication on Portuguese studies with a focus on archeology, linguistics, ethnography, and folklore.[86] This article was also part of a larger project by Adolfo Coelho, being the first installment of his 'Notas e Paralelos Floclóricos' series, or 'Notes and Folkloric Parallels', being the first tentatively academic Portuguese publication entirely devoted to the topic of Saint Cyprian traditions, legends, and literature. While the topic of Saint Cyprian had been previously mentioned by other folklorists, such as José Leite de Vasconcelos, the director of the *Revista Lusitana*, in his *Tradições Populares de Portugal* from 1882, no other publication up to that date offered the amount of information as did this by Adolfo Coelho.[87]

---

86 See COELHO - 'Notas e Parallelos Folkloricos I'. This article was republished in 1993 in the collection *Portugal de Perto* by Publicações Dom Quixote as part of a two-volume work compiling Adolfo Coelho's ethnographic studies, see COELHO - *Obra Etnográfica*, vol. 1, pp. 223-230. This more recent edition, as well as many others, can be currently digitally consulted and purchased from Etnográfica Press: https://books.openedition.org/etnograficapress/.

87 VASCONCELLOS - *Tradições Populares de Portugal*, p. 305-6.

Adolfo Coelho's work, as a whole, should be looked at as firstly a product of its time, and within this, his own idiosyncratic preoccupations and the very conception he had of his activities as a self-styled and self-taught scholar. Primarily among his preoccupations was education, which, teamed with his ethnographic and folkloric work, aimed at exploring and understanding the Portuguese people, their character, and their faults in order to find remedies for their ills.[88] This reflected itself in his collection and study of folk tales as a means of transmission of knowledge, being one of the first to publish English translations of such Portuguese source material.[89]

His approach to such topics seems to gradually evolve towards comparative models of Indo-European diffusion with an Orientalizing tendency, with the idea of independent generation of cultures being a constant struggle for him.[90] Perhaps due to this, Adolfo Coelho's preoccupations were not divorced from nineteenth-century romantic ideas on patriotism and national identity and his urge to regenerate what he saw as Portuguese national decay. As such, he was not without political ambitions, being a collaborator of Teófilo Braga, another fundamental ethnographer of the late nineteenth and early twentieth century who would eventually become the second president of the first Portuguese Republic. As such, Adolfo Coelho would become one of the participants of the historical *Conferências do Casino*, a series of revolutionary and pro-democracy talks by the intellectual group *Geração de 70*.[91]

---

88 CORREIA - 'Adolfo Coelho', p. 1-2, 7.

89 See COELHO - *Tales of Old Lusitania*.

90 LEAL - 'Prefácio', p. 20-1, 24; LEAL - *Etnografias Portuguesas (1870 – 1970)*, p. 42.

91 LEAL - 'Prefácio', p. 26-7

Returning to his Cyprian article, all of these aspects of Adolfo Coelho's work are reflected in this one publication. Adolfo Coelho's collection of Cyprianic elements covers all aspects of folk culture, from folktales, loose incantations (mostly focused on divination), and Saint Cyprian literature. He equally collects elements from non-Portuguese sources, such as Benjamin Thorpe's *Northern Mythology*, and information from a French *Grand Grimoire/Dragon Rouge* in order to establish parameters of comparison for the Portuguese case. Yet, it should be noted that all such care is not a direct reflection of Adolfo Coelho's concern for folk culture, but rather his pedagogical preoccupation. In sum, this article ultimately amounts to a sweeping condemnation of superstitions and magic practices and literature; diagnosed ills which urged to be healed for the elevation and salvation of Portugal.[92]

Even so, besides offering rare and invaluable insights into nineteenth-century printed Portuguese *Books of Saint Cyprian* (with mentions to editions currently unknown), Adolfo Coelho's most precious contribution is his mention of an 'authentic' *Book of Saint Cyprian*.[93] He does not say when he examined this or where, only that it was entitled *Cypriani Magici Septem Horae Magicae* and that it belonged to António da Silva Túlio, curator at the Portuguese National Library, deceased four years earlier in 1884.

António da Silva Túlio was born in 1818 in Carnide (Lisbon), being an early friend of the fundamental historian Alexandre Herculano and the fundamental poet, playwright,

---

[92] See also LEITÃO - 'Searching for Cyprian in Portuguese Ethnography'.
[93] COELHO - *Obra Etnográfica*, p. 227.

and politician Almeida Garrett.[94] He started his career as a scrivener for Caldas Aulete, an important intellectual and cultural promoter, and from there he entered as an officer of the manuscript and political and cultural journal section of the Portuguese National Library in 1844, being promoted to curator of the history and literature section by 1863 and occasionally acting as library director in the absence of Mendes Leal.[95] Much like Adolfo Coelho and the ethnographers of his generation, besides history, Túlio nurtured an interest in archaeology, linguistics, and philology, gradually joining several organizations such as the *Lisbon Royal Academy of Sciences*, and founding several others, such as the *Association of Portuguese Journalists and Writers*.[96] The relationship between Adolfo Coelho and António da Silva Túlio is not well understood, but they would be familiar with each other at least as early as 1871, when both participated in a literary soirée organized by the Spanish ambassador in Portugal.[97]

---

[94] CUNHA - 'Antonio da Silva Tullio', VII:183, p. 18, VII:185, p. 38; On Herculano see LEITÃO - *Fairy Women from the Portuguese Book of Lineages of Count Dom Pedro*.

[95] CUNHA - 'Antonio da Silva Tullio', VII:184, p. 27.

[96] CUNHA - 'Antonio da Silva Tullio', VII:184, p. 27, VII:185, p. 38.

[97] NA and MPP - 'António da Silva Túlio'.

(LEFT) PORTRAIT OF FRANCISCO ADOLFO COELHO, FROM HIS IN-MEMORIAM PIECE FROM THE REVISTA DA FACULDADE DE LETRAS; (RIGHT) PORTRAIT OF ANTÓNIO DA SILVA TÚLIO FROM HIS IN-MEMORIAM PIECE FROM THE JOURNAL OCCIDENTE.[98]

While not dallying too much on the matter, Adolfo Coelho does offer a number of details regarding the physical aspects of the *Septem Horae Magicae*: it was about thirty-three folios long – not exactly a manuscript, but rather the product of a manual press, resembling a trial print for a bulk book order, and it was printed in black and red ink. Furthermore, it was written in extremely broken and difficult Latin, and the book itself was heavily damaged, 'folded in half, broken and partially ripped, by being carried in the pockets or breasts of the sorcerers', which prevented the clear reading of several sections.[99] Even still, Adolfo Coelho offered a small transcript from it in his article.

Besides this information, Adolfo Coelho offers a few considerations on the little he examined of the book, ending

---

98 *Revista da Faculdade de Letras*, I:1 (1993); *O Occidente*, VII:183 (1884), p. 17.

99 COELHO - *Obra Etnográfica*, vol. 1, p. 227-8.

up lamenting the fact that, given Túlio's death in 1884, he was unable to study this mysterious work in detail, and it eventually fell somewhere out of his reach. And indeed, apart from Adolfo Coelho's brief mention, the *Septem Horae Magicae*, the 'authentic' *Book of Saint Cyprian* of António da Silva Túlio, disappeared from all records, becoming a historical and academic mystery for the next one hundred and forty years.

When the current wave of research into the Iberian Books of Saint Cyprian restarted in the 2010s (with Félix Castro Vicente's pioneering efforts having been published in 2005), the *Septem Horae Magicae* was somewhat of a unicorn: a book known to exist, a paragraph of which had been transcribed, and a particular analysis made, but frustratingly lost to the mists of time. Several attempts to locate it were made at the Portuguese National Library, such as by the analysis of the auction catalogue of the António da Silva Túlio library in the hopes that further references to it could be found which would lead to the name of a potential buyer, but no further clues were revealed.[100] Eventually, in the context of a wider and distinct research effort intended to map the presence of magic texts and manuscripts within the Portuguese Nacional Library, the full analogue catalogue of the Manuscript and Reserved section of this institution was examined. This amounted to the individual analysis of several thousands of library index cards over the course of several months, and which, besides uncovering various manuscripts on the topics of prognostication, Sebastianism, and other esoteric subjects, on the 20th of April of 2021, rather unexpectedly produced an index card containing the library reference number for a thirty-three folio long *Septem Horae Magicas* authored by 'Cipriano (S.)'.

---

100 See SILVA - *Catalogo das Livrarias do Illustre Academico Antonio da Silva Tulio e do Distincto advogado Augusto M. de Quintella Emauz*.

The consultation request of this manuscript was immediately hit with difficulties, as it was discovered by library staff in a considerable state of decay and, at this time, only a partial visual analysis of its cover page was possible. Overall, this perfectly matched the description given by Adolfo Coelho, to the point that several breaks and omissions present in his transcript were identifiable as holes and damages in its pages, meaning that, whatever the state the manuscript was in at that exact moment, the damage it displayed was near-the-same as one hundred and forty years before, likely indicating that no significant content had been lost since Adolfo Coelho's analysis. Also, a stamp on the cover page reading 'compra' indicated that this had been bought by the Portuguese National Library during the auction of the António da Silva Túlio library, and the fact that this was not mentioned in the auction catalogue was likely due to it having been sold in bulk among the several boxes and nameless bound volumes mentioned in the catalogue. As it turned out, the *Septem Horae Magicae* had never been lost, it had simply not been added to the National Library's central catalogue and no one since, including Adolfo Coelho, had thought to search for it among the manuscript section index cards.

In the aftermath of this discovery, a concerted effort was made in conjunction with Hadean Press and the Portuguese National Library to have this manuscript pushed to the top of the restoration and digitalization queue, with all of the manuscript's information and known history being provided to the Portuguese National Library so it could be appropriately included in its current digital catalogue. By August of 2021, after almost one and a half centuries hidden from public eyes, the *Septem Horae Magicae* was restored and digitalized, and it now awaited the academic analysis Adolfo Coelho had been unable to provide.

The text of the *Septem Horae Magicae*, as Adolfo Coelho noted, seems to be written in extremely broken Latin, with possible inclusions of Greek and occasional minor instances of, potentially, Spanish. Among its several linguistic issues, there are difficult to interpret truncated and abbreviated words, many uncertain and obscure expressions, and words which seem entirely made up. This excessively complex aspect of this book, coupled with some of the extremely difficult and complicated instructions it seems to contain and the several instances of apparently missing instructions on the several magic implements it appears to mention (a consecrated pen is mentioned in fol.11v for which no consecration is provided), could indicate that this text is an elaborate historical fraud or practical joke. This is a point which is entirely impossible to clarify at this moment, and, in all honesty, it matters very little when it comes to the relevance and importance of this text in the context of Iberian Saint Cyprian-derived literature.

Despite these difficulties, a translation was produced, and the resulting text, even though it is written in contemporary English, is still extremely complicated and ambiguous, a fact only made worse by the several blocks which have been lost to damage. Overall, even though a translation was produced, the resulting text cannot be said to be more than a linguistically-informed interpretation, and alternative views and opinions are surely possible.

From my best interpretation, the *Septem Horae Magicae* can be divided into five different parts. The first of these, roughly contained between fol.2r and fol.4v, can be considered as an introduction, and in it one is given the information that this is a book of Cyprian and of 'Locifuge Refocele', meant for the magic discovery of treasure.[101] This immediately inserts

---

101 BNP, Manuscritos Reservados, *Cypriani Magjcj Septem Horae Magicae, Editae ab ipso Bernae 154...*, MSS. 174, n. 155, fol.2r.

this book into the intersection of *Grand Grimoire* and Iberian Saint Cyprian material. As mentioned, the influence of this grimoire is much more visible in the Spanish expressions of the Cyprian literary tradition, suggesting Spain as the origin of this manuscript, a hypothesis given further weight by what appear to be small inclusions of Spanish in its text. However, as already attested, *Grand Grimoire* incursions are not unknown in the Portuguese case.

Among the several relevant names of late-nineteenth and early-twentieth century ethnography, another which should not be missed, particularly when discussing the general topic of magic treasure hunting (be it Cyprian-related or not) is that of Francisco Martins Sarmento. While primarily an archeologist, Sarmento paid considerable attention to the phenomenon of treasure hunting, mostly due to two opposing reasons. The first was that he considered treasure hunting literature as a legitimate source for archaeological research, particularly the several manuscript treasure lists which, until the mid-twentieth century, were relatively common in northern Portugal, and usually referred to as *tombos* or *roteiros*. On par with this, Sarmento was also an attentive examiner of would-be treasure hunters, given that these would, with relative frequence, be behind the destruction of archeological sites in their search for buried riches. As such, besides having produced at least one article on the subject,[102] among Sarmento's personal notebooks one can find descriptions of two *Books of Saint Cyprian* he examined during his expeditions and which he refers to by the titles of *Pai Santo: Livro de S. Cipriano*, or *Holy Father: Book of St. Cyprian* and *Livro do Rei S. Cipriano*, or *Book of King St. Cyprian*.[103]

---

102 See SARMENTO - 'A Proposito dos «Roteiros de Thesouros»'.
103 See LEITÃO - *Opuscula Cypriani*, p. 287-309.

PORTRAIT OF FRANCISCO MARTINS SARMENTO FROM HIS IN-MEMORIAM PIECE
FROM THE *JOURNAL OCCIDENTE*.[104]

The notes Sarmento took on these two books, while enlightening of several aspects of the Saint Cyprian tradition in the nineteenth century, are still rather omissive; namely, it is uncertain if these were printed or manuscript and to whom they belonged. Still, we are given assurance they were real by the several block transcriptions Sarmento provides, and analysis reveals that both these books were entirely distinct in their contents, but were otherwise similar in terms of conception and purpose.

---

104 *O Occidente*, XXII:744 (1899), p. 189.

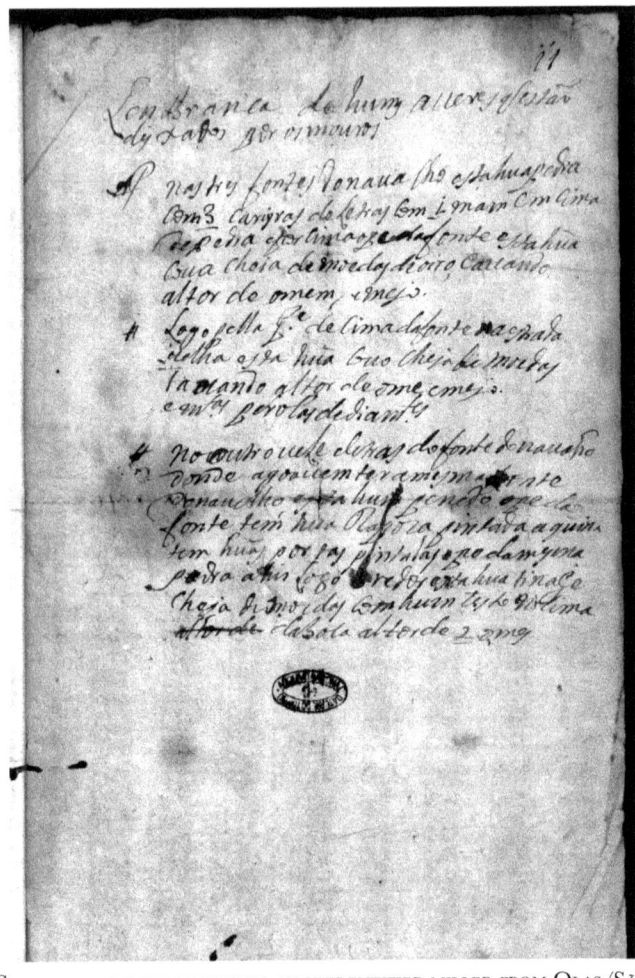

Small roteiro belonging to an unidentified miller from Olas (São João da Pesqueira), 1740, entitled *Lembrança de huns averes que estão deixados por os mouros*, or *Memory of some belongings which are left by the moors*.[105]

---

[105] ANTT, Tribunal do Santo Ofício, Inquisição de Coimbra, Promotor, Livro n°378, fol.11r; PT/TT/TSO-IC/026/0378, Imagem cedida pelo ANTT.

The *Holy Father* was composed of apparently three parts. The first of these is a rather short *roteiro*, presenting two descriptions of treasure locations. Following this, the second part and likely the most relevant, is an adaptation of the spirit summoning procedures of *The Grimoire of Pope Honorius*, a late-seventeenth century French magic book likely derived from the *Sworn Book of Honorius*, a medieval grimoire with mentions going back to the first half of the thirteenth century.[106] From here the *Holy Father* presented either a magic circle or the instructions to create one, derived from the pseudo-Abano *Heptameron* and which repurposes the previous *Honorius* content as a ritual for the finding of treasure. In total, the *Holy Father* seems to be a 'composite' magic book, made from sections of several non-Iberian grimoires woven together as a treasure hunting manual, which, in the Portuguese context, made it identifiable as a Book of Saint Cyprian.[107]

The *Book of King St. Cyprian* is a similar object, but instead of an 'importation' of *Honorius* and *Heptameron* material, it is an adaptation of the *Grand Grimoire* and once again meant for the sole purpose of treasure hunting. Not only this, but the *Book of King St. Cyprian* also possessed a second part, composed of other loose magical procedures and where one can also find a second method for the disenchantment of treasure which is very much similar to sections of MS. 2559 from the University of Coimbra, indicating some sort of genealogical relation between these two books.[108]

On par with these two references, the researcher Félix Castro Vicente has recently located an obscure printed Book

---

106 DAVIES, Owen - *Grimoires*, p. 34.

107 SMS, Manuscritos, Série: *Citânia e Sabroso*, Caderno 37, p. 10-6.

108 SMS, Manuscritos, Série: *Citânia e Sabroso*, Caderno 37, p. 17-30; BGUC, Reservados, *[Orações Várias para Afugentar o Demonio]*, n.d., MS. 2559, fol.27v.

of Saint Cyprian entitled *El Verdadero Libro de San Ciprian*, or *The True Book of Saint Cyprian*, romantically found among religious literature in a Saint Cyprian church in the vicinity of Toledo. Besides its own intrinsic relevance and interest, this newly discovered book complements this picture of what appears to be a particular moment of the tradition of the Books of Saint Cyprian, where they became the recipient of multiple influences from non-Iberian sources and magic books. While the analysis of this Toledo *True Book of Saint Cyprian* is still rudimentary, it seems to open with a repurpose of material from the *Heptameron* which, after the conjuration of the spirits of the week, is pasted together with the invocation of Lucifer from the *Grand Grimoire*, reframing the previous *Heptameron* section as, once again, a treasure hunting ritual. Interestingly, while this section in the 'original' *Grand Grimoire* does not mention the name of the spirit Lucifuge Rofocale, instead asking Lucifer to end his envoy Astaroth to the spirit summoner, in the Toledo *The True Book of Saint Cyprian* he is nonetheless included in this section as the two apparently distinct spirit names of Lucefuge and Rofocale.[109] Another variation to the *Grand Grimoire* ritual formality present here is the substitution of the blasting rod, meant for the constraint and forceful handling of spirits, with a priestly stole, further tying it to the local Iberian culture of magic treasure hunting. Additionally, this *Grand Grimoire* material is once again broken by an extremely unusual and long Cyprian prayer which, while occasionally sharing some structural elements with the common Prayer of Saint Cyprian, deviates from it considerably, including mentions to Lucifer, Lucefuge, and Rofocale, and being explicitly tailored for treasure hunting

---

109 ACV, ANON. - *El Verdadero Libro de San Ciprian*. n.p.: n.d., p. 32-3.

and identifying its reader as a priest.[110]

All of this is to say that the mention of Lucifuge in the *Septem Horae Magicae* is logical and contextually valid for an early-nineteenth century Cyprian book, and these four instances, collectively, describe a very specific moment of the Iberian Saint Cyprian tradition which is only now becoming clear. Given the overwhelming conception of Cyprian books as treasure hunting literature since the Iberian eighteenth century, and Saint Cyprian as the patron of treasure hunting, this shift towards *Grand Grimoire* methodologies in the late-eighteenth and early-nineteenth century seems to also place the spirit Lucifuge Rofocale as a central Iberian treasure guardian, making him a direct magic rival and antagonist/partner to Cyprian in the world of treasure hunting. One is the keeper of treasures, the other the dispensator of hidden riches.

The introductory section of the *Septem Horae Magicae* continues with brief and general instructions for the appropriate practice of magic, and a mention of the planetary hours.[111] Finally, its treasure hunting purpose is further clarified by the mention of Moorish treasure, which this book is meant to magically disenchant, which then leads back to the notion of the treasure guardian and folkloric figure of the *moura encantada*.

From a culturally contextual position, the notion of buried treasure in the Iberian Peninsula tends to be that of Moorish treasure, being associated with the notion Iberians (be they medieval, early modern, modern, or contemporary) have that the territory they inhabit was, at some point in the past, the possession of a religiously and (partially) ethnically distinct people.[112] Thus, buried treasures are taken to be the

---

110 ACV, ANON. - *El Verdadero Libro de San Ciprian*. n.p.: n.d., p. 48.

111 BNP, Manuscritos Reservados, *Cypriani Magjcj Septem Horae Magicae, Editae ab ipso Bernae 154…*, MSS. 174, n. 155, fol.2v, fol.4r.

112 PARAFITA - *A Mitologia dos Mouros*, p. 88-9.

riches left behind by the previous Muslim rulers and the general population of the Umayyad Caliphate during the period of the *Reconquista*. This general notion holds true in both purely folk cultural environments and learned ones, as attested by the twelfth century *Codex Calixtinus*, a pilgrim's guide to the road of Saint James which mentions Galicia as a land 'rich in gold and silver, fabrics and wild pelts, and in other riches, and overall Saracen treasure'.[113] This, for the inhabitants of this geographic and cultural space, generates a 'mixed reality' between historical accounts and mythical fabulations surrounding the foundational narratives of the several Iberian Christian kingdoms and the movement of the *Reconquista* as a whole, and which is eventually codified in various culturally edifying narratives.[114] The stark religious and racial distinction (often more imaginary than real) drawn in the Iberian 'collective imaginary' between Christians, as the current rulers of this territory, and Moors, as the previous rulers, effectively pushes the latter into a realm of chronological murkiness, associating their name and constructed image with all of the elements within the local landscape which cannot be accurately located within the collective memory of known historical time.

This means that buried treasure, riches left behind by other cultures and civilizations, unknown or unusual structures such as megalithic monuments, Roman or early medieval ruins, caverns, water basins or strange rock formations (equally the common targets of treasure hunters in the rest of Europe), become associated with the notion of the 'Moor' not so much as an ancestor but as a radical outsider and antagonist to Christian culture and society, making them

---

113 SUÁREZ LÓPEZ - *Tesoros, Ayalgas y Chalgueiros*, p. 17.

114 PARAFITA - *A Mitologia dos Mouros*, p. 67.

into a sort of cosmological 'other'.[115] This makes the very notion and idea of previous Muslim inhabitants of Iberia not that of a merely distinct people or culture who just happened to live in these regions somewhere in the past, but a mythical people of pre- or anti-cosmic connotations, frequently in league with the Devil and collectively referred to as *mouros* or *mouras*, occasionally mentioned as *encantados*, or enchanted.[116]

The notion of *encanto* is of primary relevance for the understanding of *mouras* and the notions of buried treasure and folk treasure hunting in Iberia. Primarily, this word indicates a state of being which can be seen to be imposed not only upon individuals but also objects, locations, and animals. As noted by Alexandre Parafita, to be *encantado* means to be forced into an 'inferior state'.[117] Something, while under an *encanto*, can change form or substance, be placed under profoundly restricting taboos and modes of action, or be absolutely subjected to another's will. Both objects and individuals, when under an *encanto*, can also acquire zoomorphic characteristics, revealing themselves in the forms of animals. In the case of *mouras*, the overwhelming majority of narratives describe them as being *encantadas* under the form of snakes, serpents, or monstrous woman-snake hybrids.[118] More complex than just a simple transformation and subjugation, an individual or object under an *encanto* exists in a continuous state of in-betweenness, neither living nor dead. This kind of suspended existence makes them manifest as a kind of ghost or immaterial spirit, although, according to the general conception of *encanto*, they are not dead but are simply trapped in a state of suspension.

---

115 PARAFITA - *A Mitologia dos Mouros*, p. 126-7, 97-8.
116 PARAFITA - *A Mitologia dos Mouros*, p. 85.
117 PARAFITA - *A Mitologia dos Mouros*, p. 139-40.
118 PARAFITA - *A Mitologia dos Mouros*, p. 141.

Importantly, while in the Iberian context *mouras* tend to be portrayed as rather passive entities, there are rare Inquisition mentions of them as active and intrusive spirits, capable of entering into human bodies as serpents and giving rise to a situation of possession, meaning that the state of *encanto* is not solely one of reactivity.[119]

From folk sources, the state of *encanto* can be broken by a third party if they abide by and follow certain rules and rituals, which tend to be ingrained and implicit within each different treasure and *moura* folk narrative, there being no general and monolithic method of *desencanto*, or disenchantment. *Desencanto* might need to be done at particular times and hours (midnight, midday, and St. John's Eve are common references), it might require particular objects, the fulfillment of time-dependent taboos by the would-be disenchanter, the breaking of social norms or the fulfilling of symbolic favors.[120] From a folk treasure hunting perspective, the act or ritual of *desencanto* is, effectively, the cultural-specific ritual for magic treasure hunting, bringing not only the buried treasure out of its immaterial transitional state, but equally releasing its potential guardian, the *moura*, from its imprisoned state. Alternatively, and as expressed by the *Septem Horae Magicae*, *moura* and treasure disenchantment can be done by recourse to a specialized learned or para-learned magic book carrying its own general treasure hunting ritual, applicable to any and all circumstances where a treasure or a *moura* might be thought to exist. In fact, such a ritual does not need to be sought in a *moura-* or Iberian-specific text; there are records of Iberian treasure hunters resorting to wider-reaching learned magic texts, such as *Claviculas Salomonis*, in order to

---

119 RIBEIRO - *O Auto dos Místicos*, p. 456, 496-7.

120 See PARAFITA - *A Mitologia dos Mouros*, p. 148-53.

attempt to banish *mouras*.[121] In sum, the *Septem Horae Magicae*, by having the disenchantment of *moura* treasure placed as its central purpose, besides firmly anchoring it in the local Iberian culture of treasure hunting in both its learned and folk expressions, also implies *mouras* to be subservient to Lucifuge, effectively operating a 'folklorization' of this spirit.

The *Septem Horae Magicae*'s second part, from fol.4v to fol.7v continues with instructions for the construction of what it seems to refer to as a 'talisman' (uncertain translation). This is a complex object composed of wooden staves from various trees (cypress, cinnamon, beech and oak), cut during specific days and planetary hours and nailed together with the teeth of specific animals (wolves and donkeys). In total, seven of these 'talismans' should be produced, and another olive wood stave fashioned in such a way as to go through all the 'talismans' so that they may rotate independently of each other with this stave as their central axis. There are also instructions for the attachment of a blackbird's head and a cat's eye to this central stave, and to produce a cord to somehow hang all of this. The size of these elements is substantial, with each 'talisman' being a square with a 50-inch side and the central olive wood stave 47 inches in length (127 and 119,38 centimeters respectively, should our translation be accurate). At the end of this section there is a recipe for an apparent oil or resin of unclear purpose, but it might be meant to a grease the 'talismans' or simply the cord attached to this construction.

The third section of the manuscript, from fol.7v to fol.12v, seems to offer instructions for the performance of a pact with Lucifuge. Included here are what appear to be instructions for a magic circle and recipes for a magic candle

---

121 See ANTT, Tribunal do Santo Oficio, Inquisição de Lisboa, Processos, n°2393, fol.44r.

and anointing oil. Part of the wording of this pact appears to be a denial of sacred or divine magic and authority. This stands as a fundamental point in the described system, and it clearly breaks with the standard spirit evocation methods of Solomonic magic, in which the *Grand Grimoire* inserts itself. The instructions concerning this pact are mostly understandable, which, if for nothing else, makes this book stand as an extremely interesting and valuable resource for the understanding of diabolical pacts in early-nineteenth century Iberia.

The fourth part, from fol.13r to fol.15v, seems to be the specific instructions to work the 'talisman' and discover treasure. While this is extremely ambiguous, an interpretation of this section might be that this 'talisman' is supposed to be hung in the vicinity of a treasure, which should be indicated by some sort of movement of the blackbird head attached to the central stave of the 'talisman'. This step, besides the attention given to the 'talisman', given the explicitly diabolical nature of the text and its rejection of sacred magic and divine authority, can easily be classified as a black mass, as the operator seems to be instructed to consume a host (possibly with a chalice of wine) and recite psalms from a Bible fumigated with a specific incense, which is also described. At the culmination of the ritual, it is suggested that the 'talisman' should be destroyed, being cast down 'from on high'.

Finally, the *Septem Horae Magicae* ends with a long list of psalms meant to be read (likely from the consecrated Bible, see appendix) at various planetary hours as the disenchantment ritual continues throughout the night, offering also occasional instructions for specific invocations and details regarding the performance of the black mass, such as in fol.31r-v. It is this section which likely names the entirety of the book.

The text is finally closed with a handwritten signature of Cyprian (a reduced version of which is also present in most pages), a diagram which seems to be a representation of the 'talisman' and a final note referring to the supposed functioning of the 'talisman' in the detection of treasure.

Concluding Remarks

What follows is the first printed publication of the *Cypriani Magici Septem Horae Magicae*; its first public exposition since its 1888 preshow. Its history is largely unknown, its authorship unnamed, its purpose obscure. As a scholar of magic, had I not seen it for myself on the 20th of April in 2021, should anyone describe such a Book of Saint Cyprian to me, I would be quick to call them liars. Magic texts are, by definition, irreverent texts within normalized 'Western' society and academic culture, but this one is irreverent even by the standards of a magic text. As stated at the opening of this introduction, it poses more question than it answers.

As such, it is impossible to claim any finality or untouchable veracity to anything written about it here. However, having found this text, I believe it to be my job to make it available to all those interested, and they should be given a type of access to it which might allow for future alternatives or divergent interpretations. As such, in the presentation of the *Septem Horae Magicae*, what will be firstly given is the facsimile digitalization of this text created by the Portuguese National Library staff (the same digitalization which can be consulted today on the library's website). Following this is a transcription of the text and, following this, its translation, both originally produced by Brian Johnson,[122] and then subsequently tentatively amended and 'smoothed over' for comprehension purposes. The resulting text is, admittedly, very far from comprehensive, but I honestly do

---

122 Author and translator of *Necromancy in the Medici Library*, published by Hadean Press (2019).

not believe that to be so much our fault but rather an intrinsic characteristic of the text. Following this, a minor appendix is offered containing all the psalms mentioned in the text.

With this, while *Septem Horae Magicae* might still hide its mysteries, it cannot hide itself anymore.

Cypriani Magici
Septem Horae Magicae

Facsimile

Cypriani Magici Septem Horae Magicae Facsimile

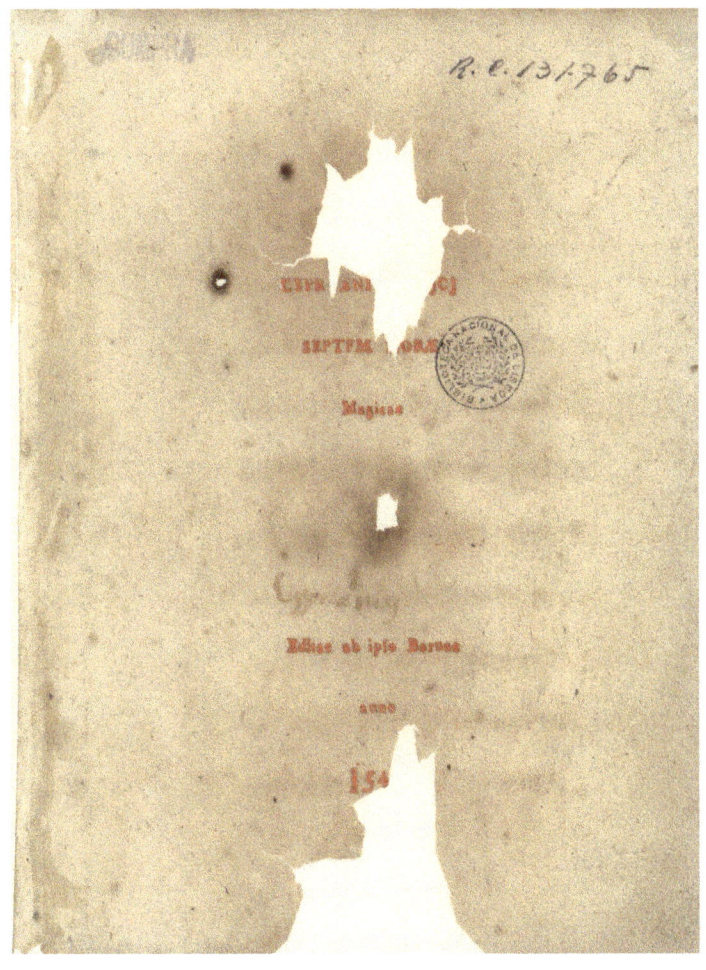

folio 0r.

folio 0v.

Cypriani Magici Septem Horae Magicae Facsimile

folio 1r.

folio 1v.

folio 2r.

folio 2v.

folio 3r.

folio 3v.

folio 4r.

folio 4v.

Cypriani Magici Septem Horae Magicae Facsimile

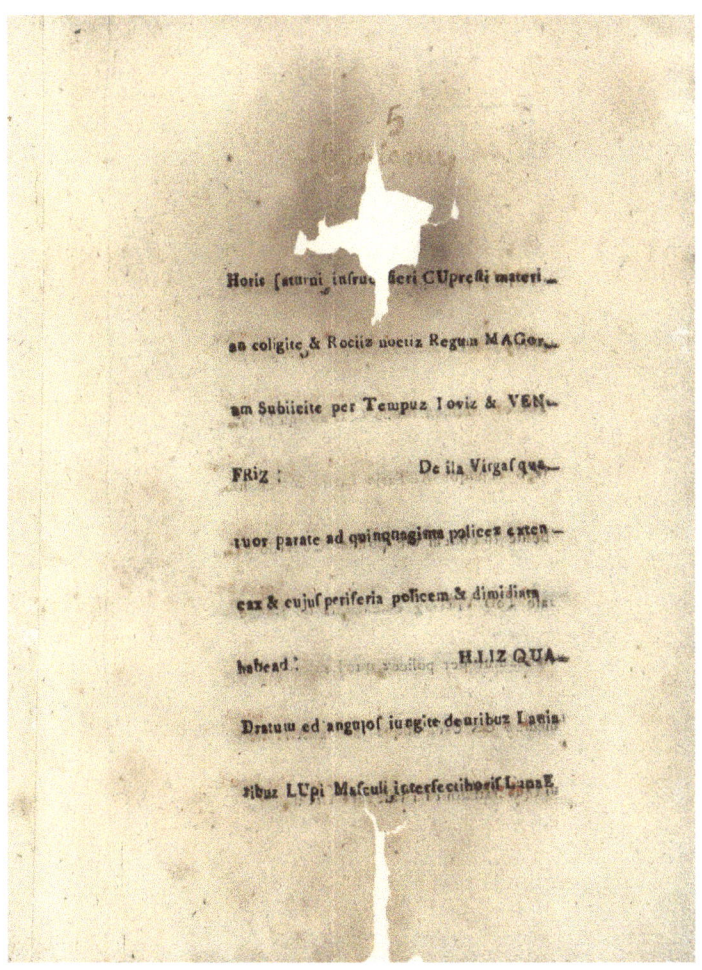

Horis Saturni instrue fieri CUpreßi materi-

aa coligite & Rociis noctis Regum MAGor-

am Subiicite per Tempus Iovis & VEN-

FRIZ: De illa Virgas qua-

tuor parate ad quinquaginta polices exten-

cax & cujus periferia policem & dimidium

habead: HIIZ QUA-

Dratum ed angulos iuegite deuribus Lacia-

ribus LUpi Masculi interfectihorif LunaE

folio 5r.

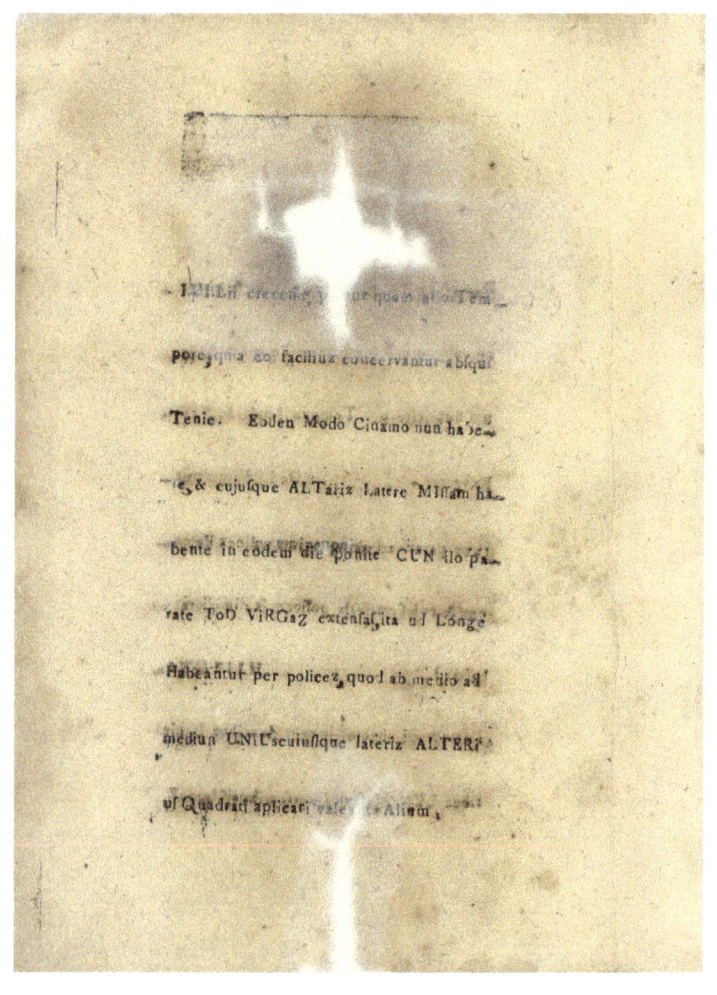

folio 5v.

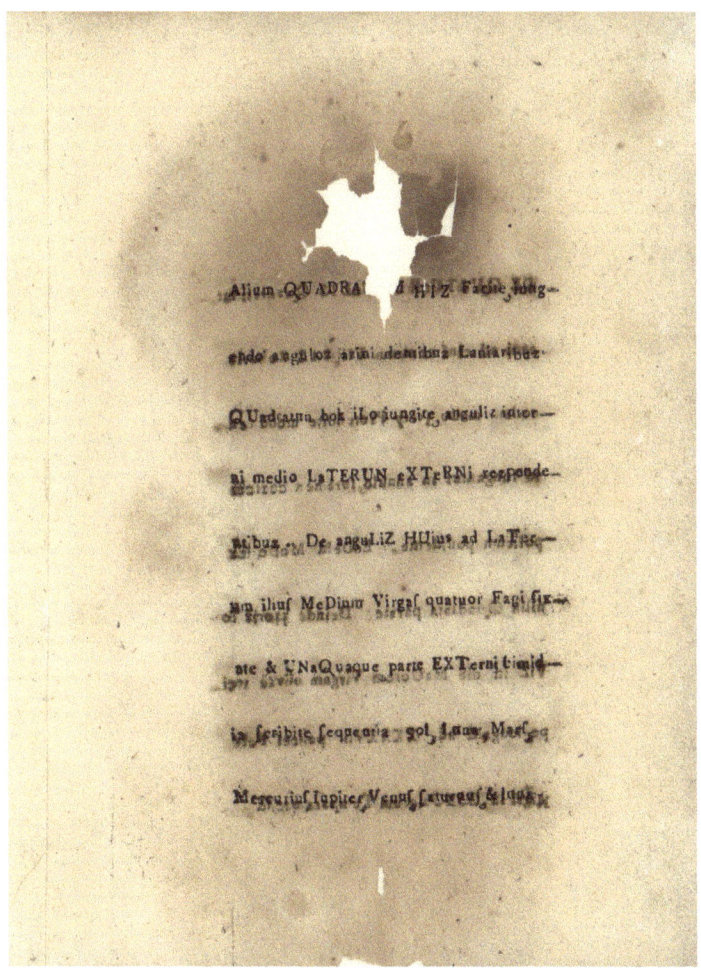

folio 6r.

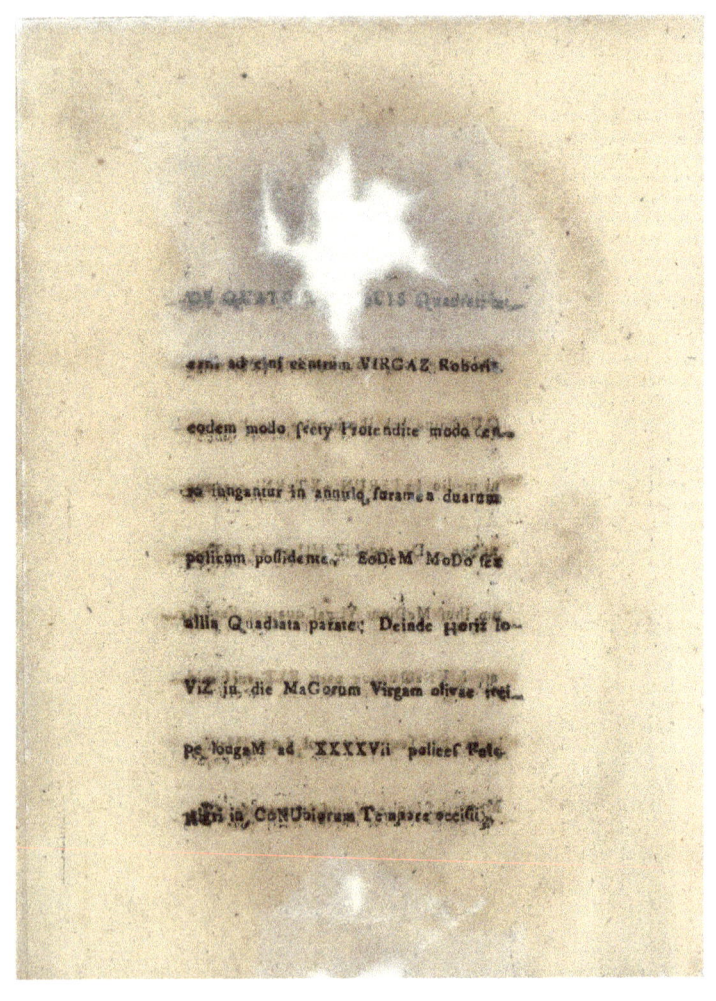

folio 6v.

folio 7r.

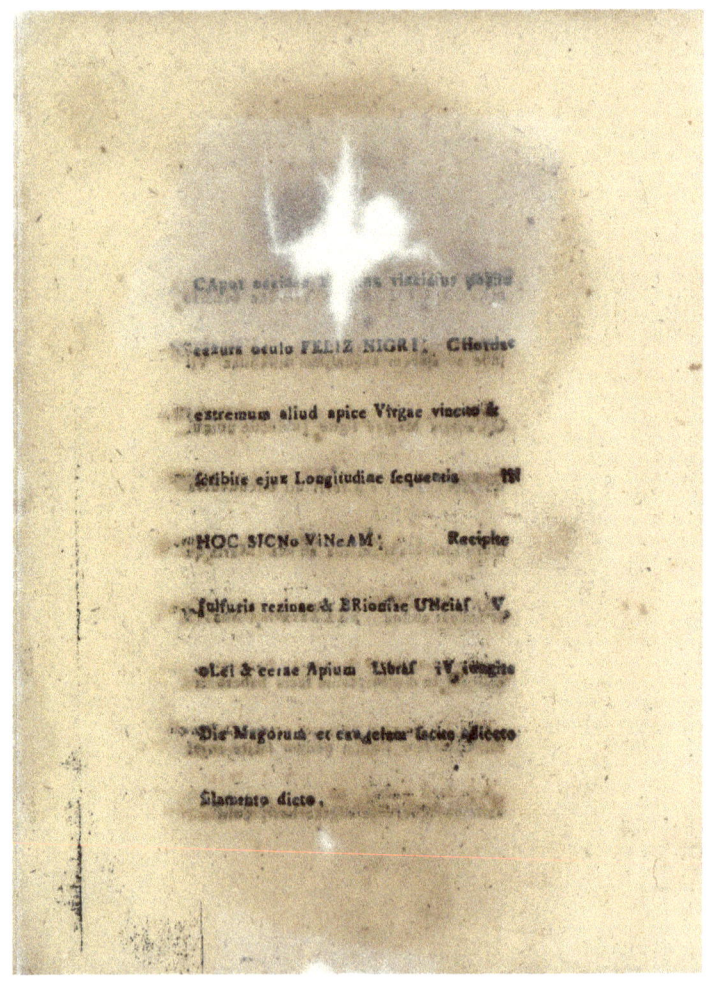

folio 7v.

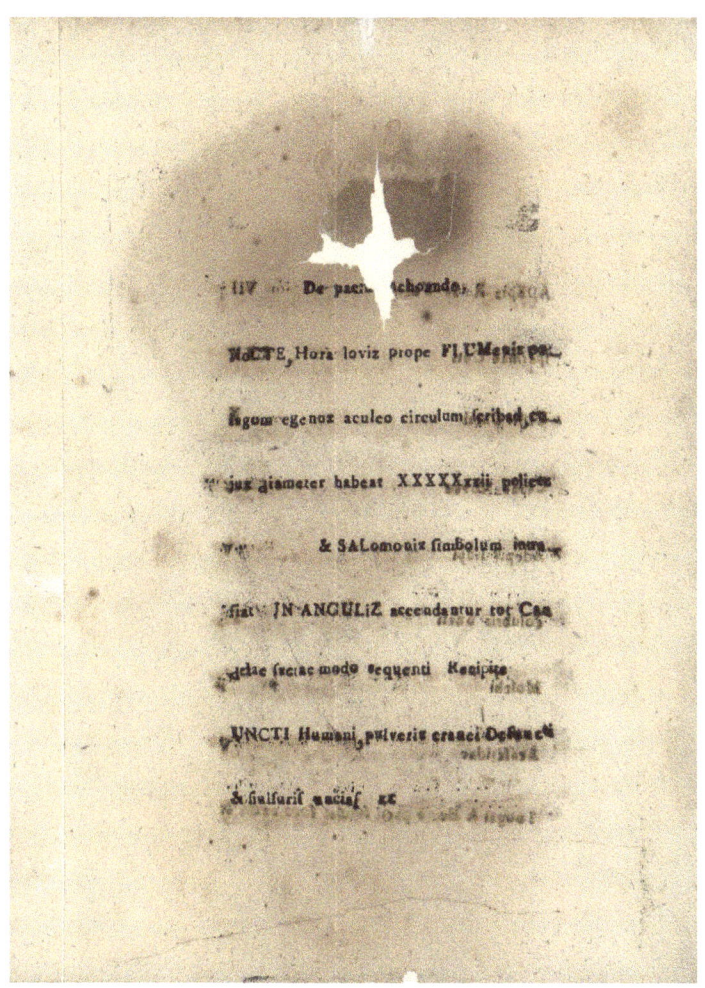

folio 8r.

folio 8v.

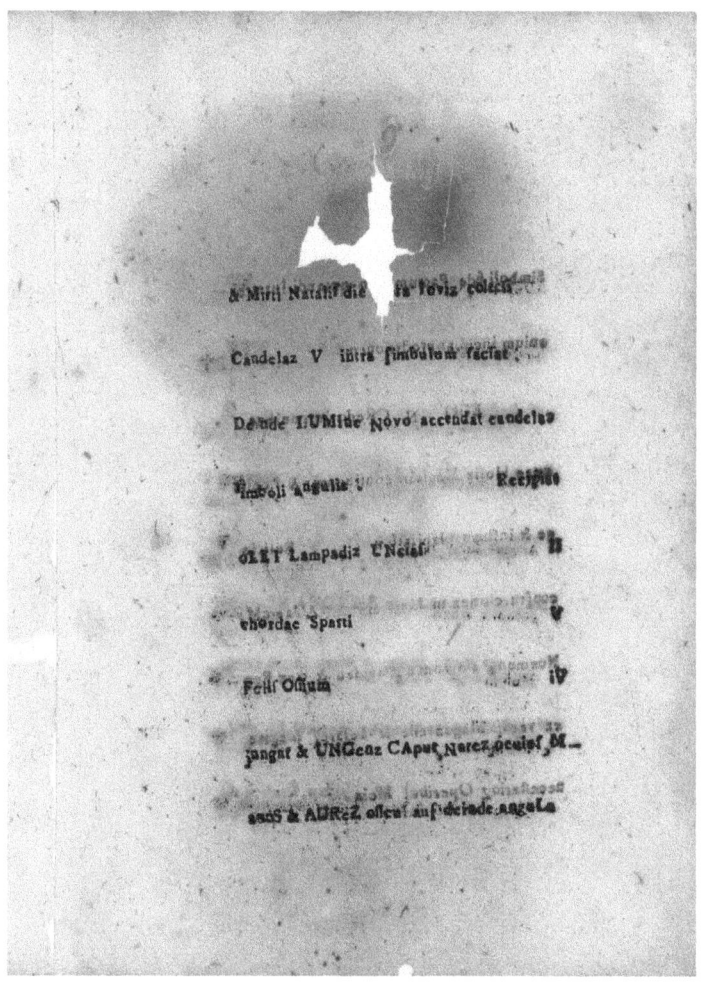

folio 9r.

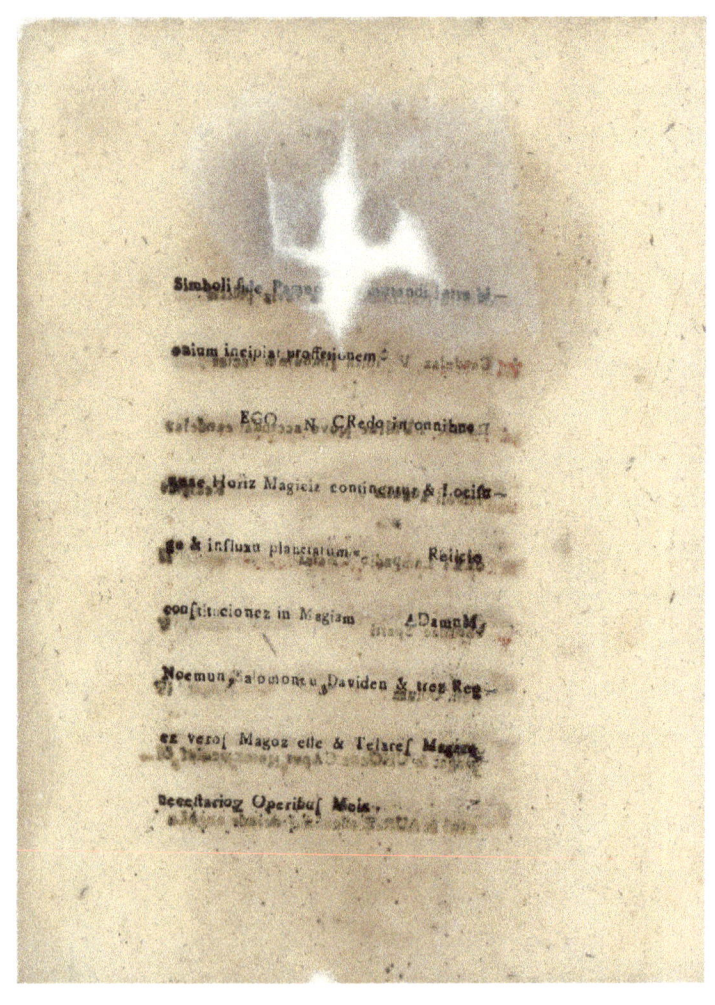

folio 9v.

folio 10r.

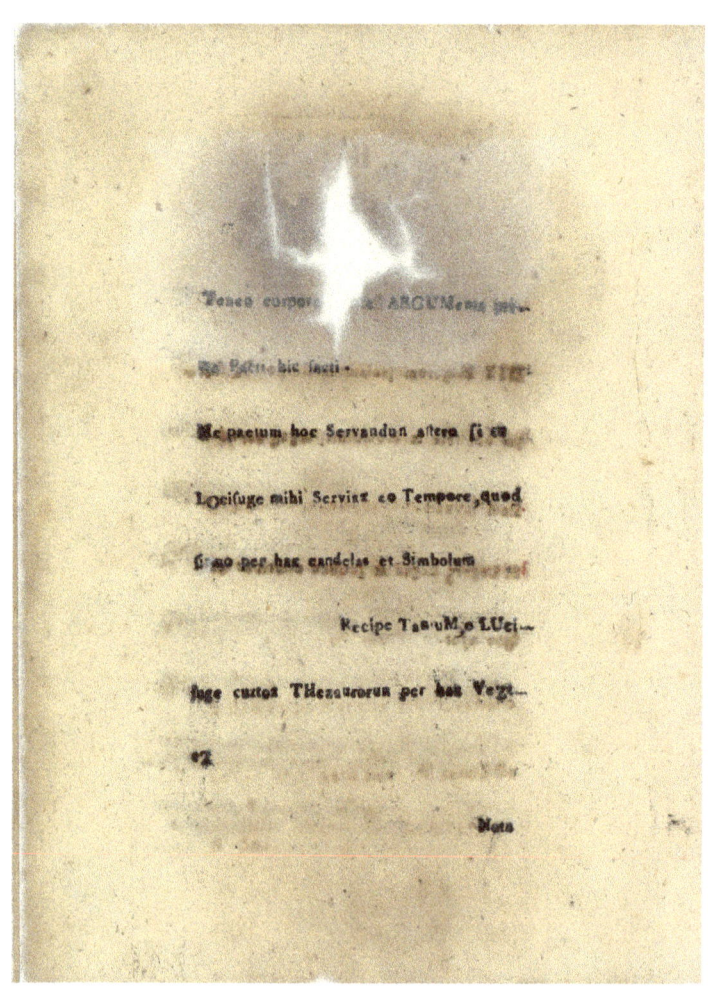

folio 10v.

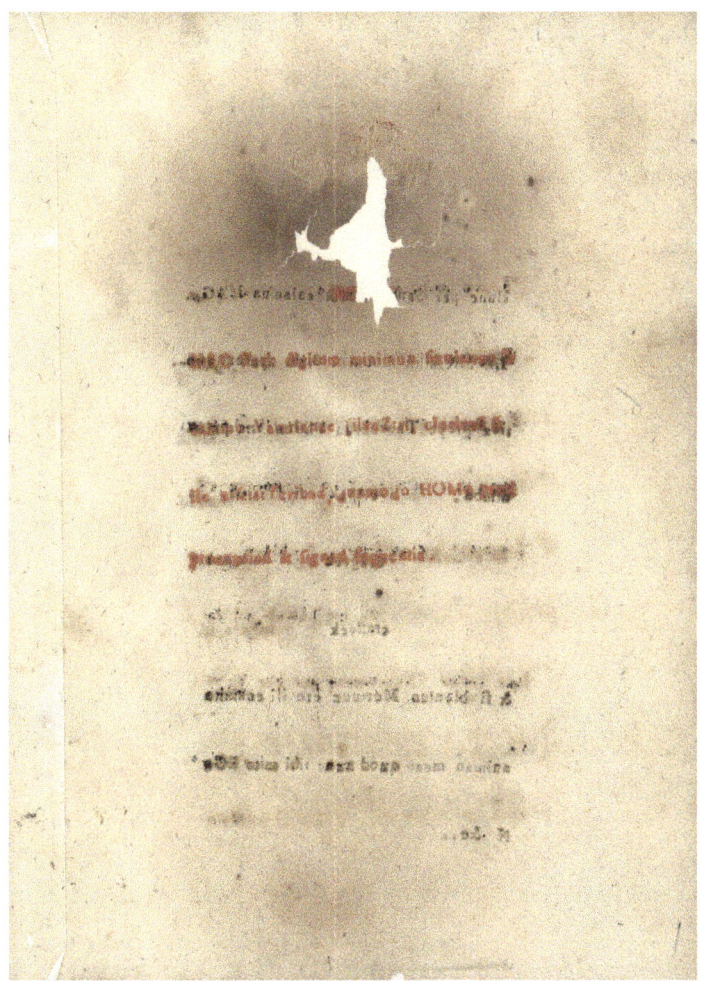

folio 11r.

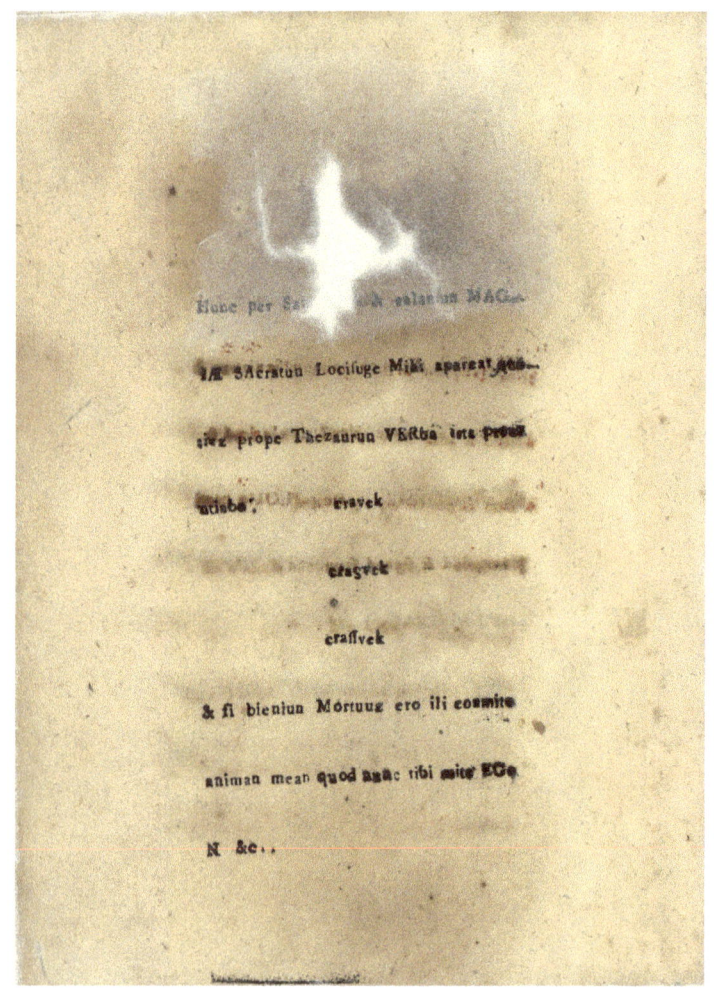

folio 11v.

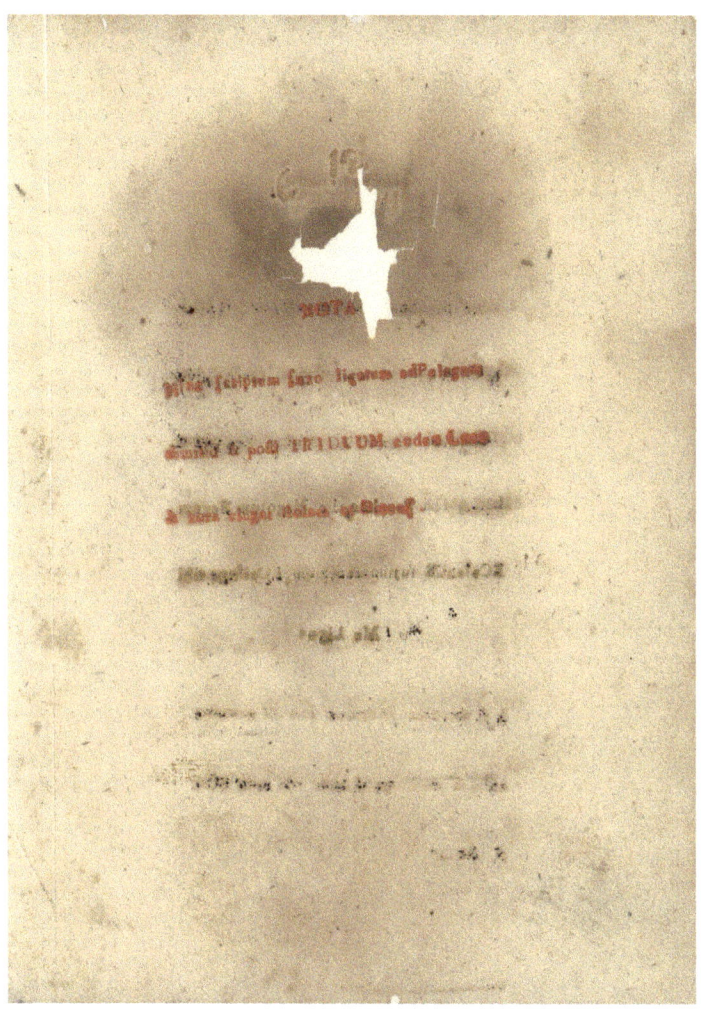

folio 12r.

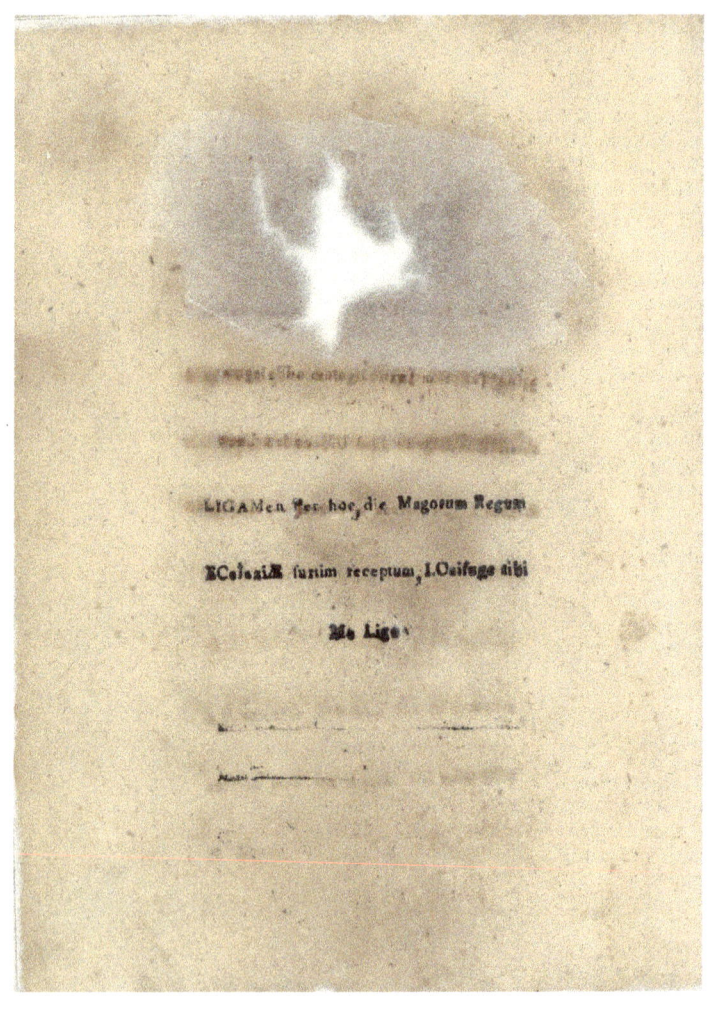

folio 12v.

folio 13r.

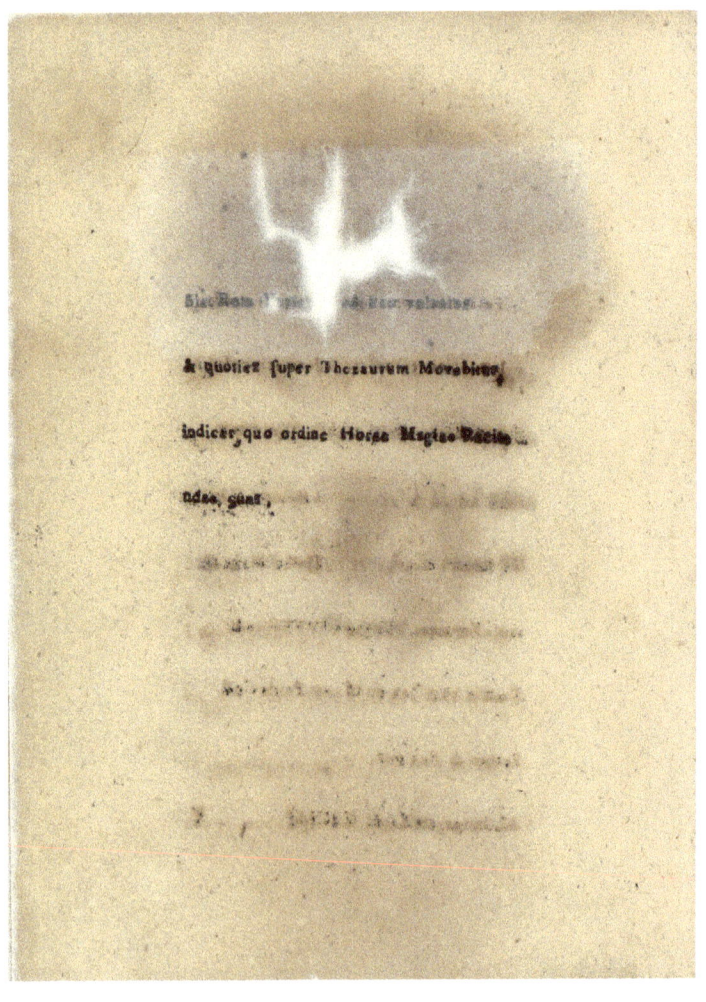

folio 13v.

Cypriani Magici Septem Horae Magicae Facsimile

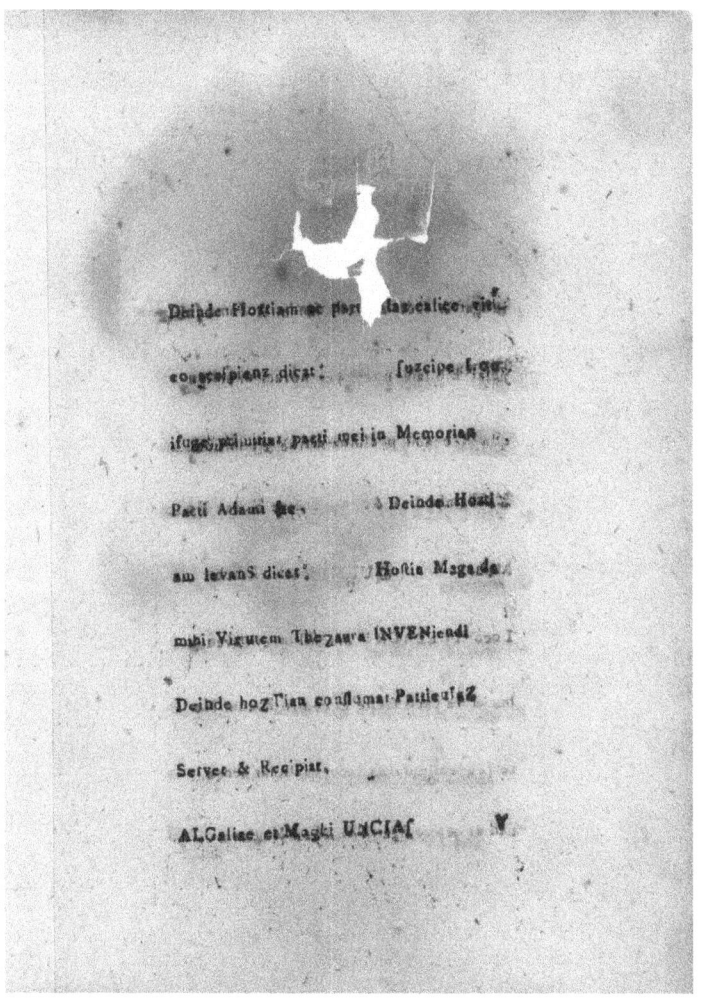

folio 14r.

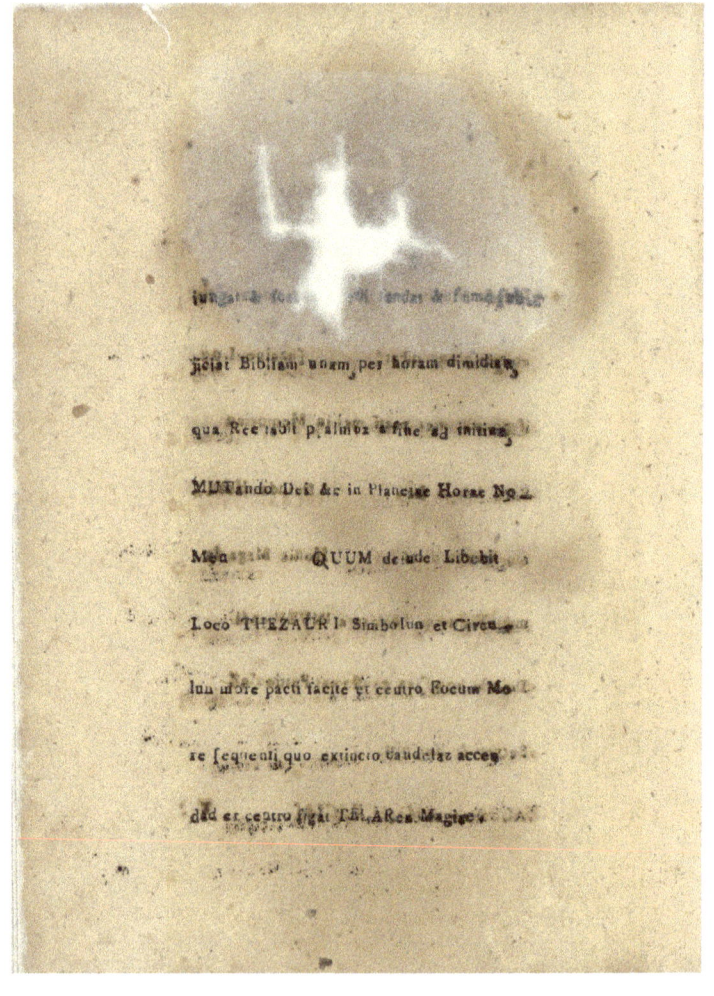

folio 14v.

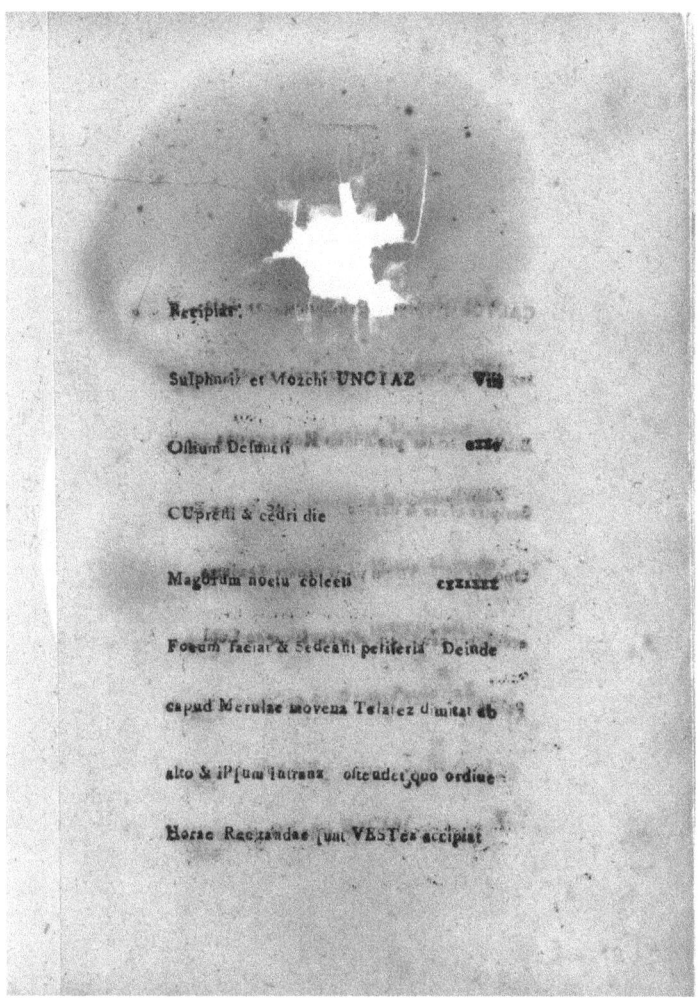

folio 15r.

folio 15v.

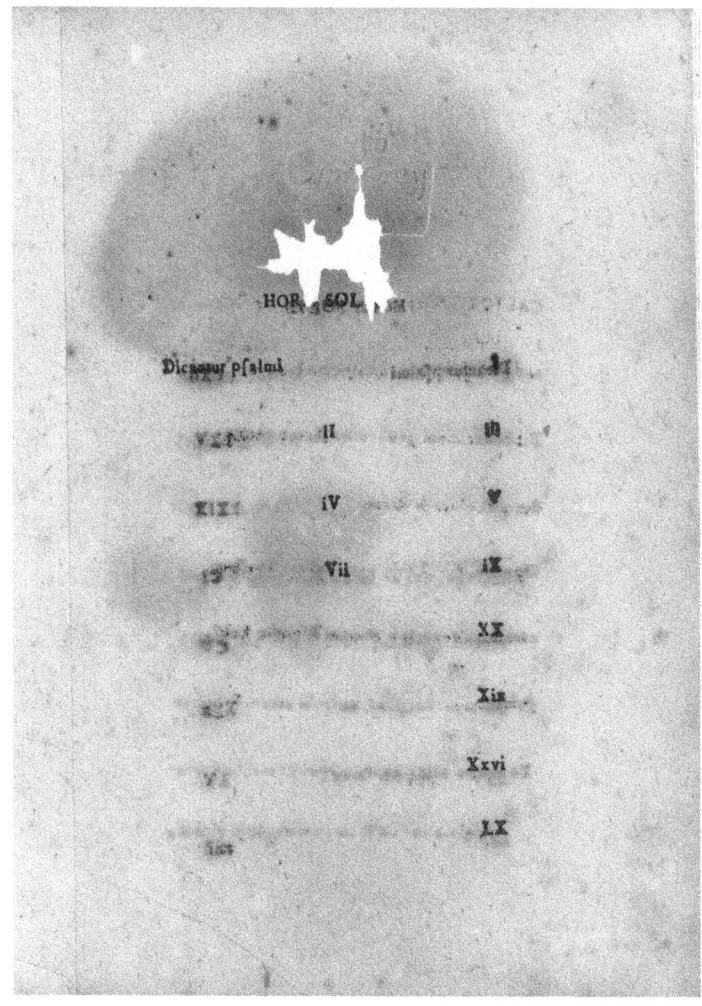

folio 16r.

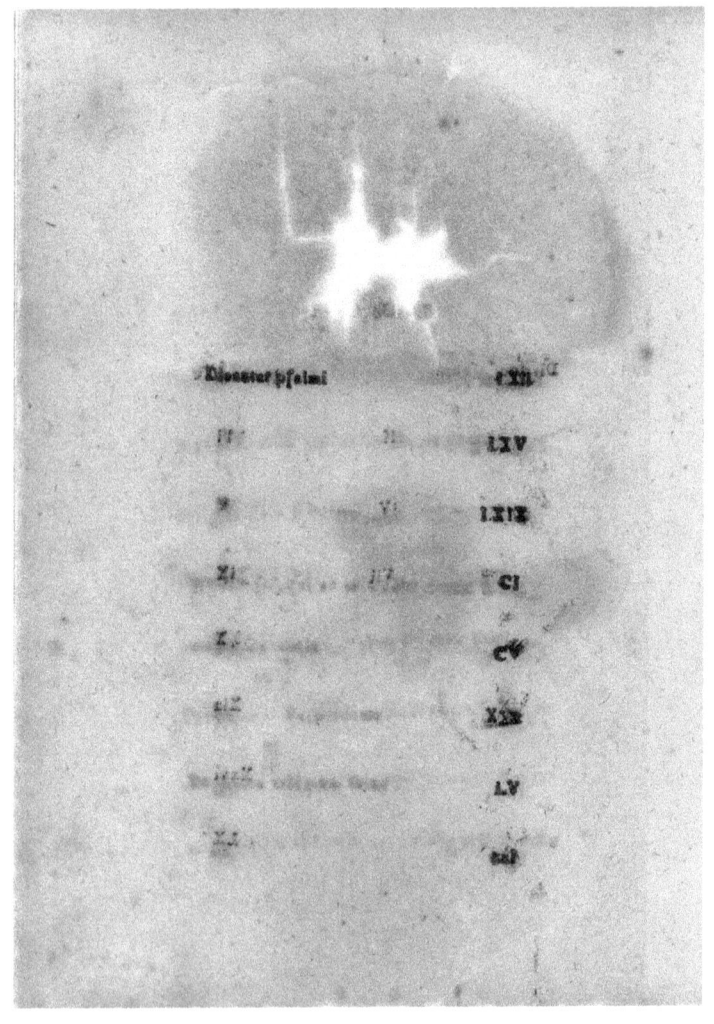

folio 16v.

Cypriani Magici Septem Horae Magicae Facsimile

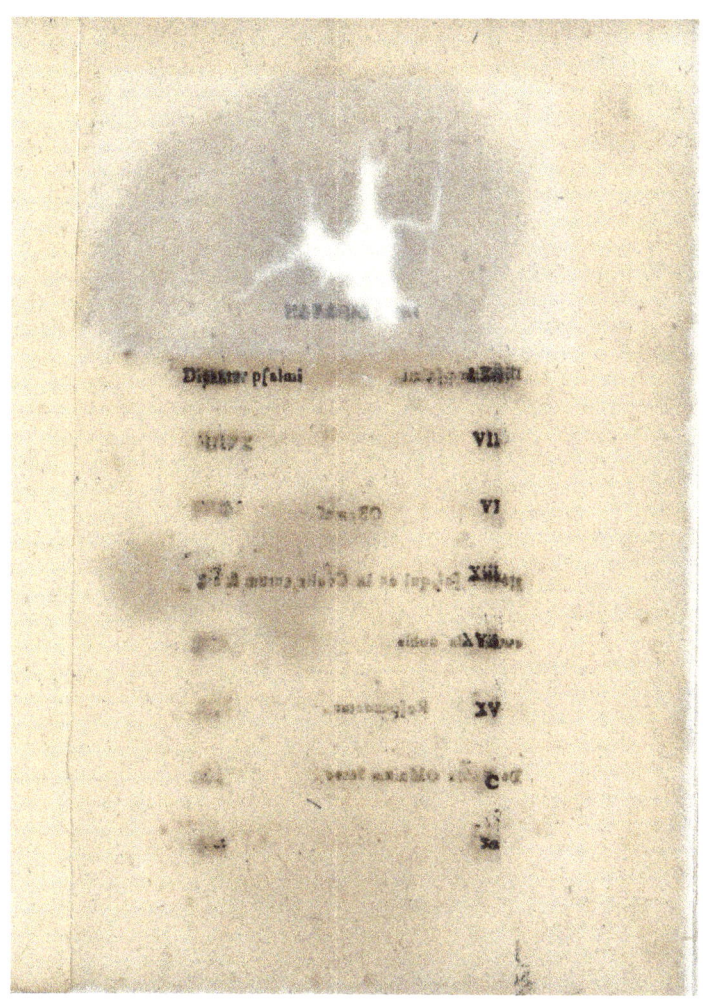

folio 17r.

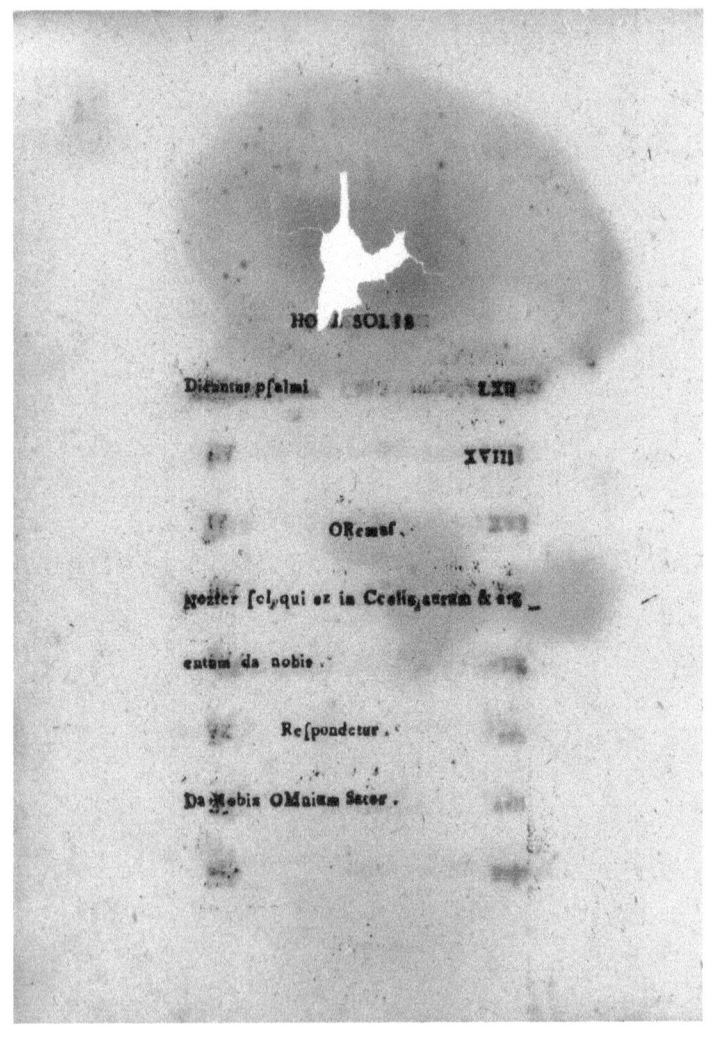

folio 17v.

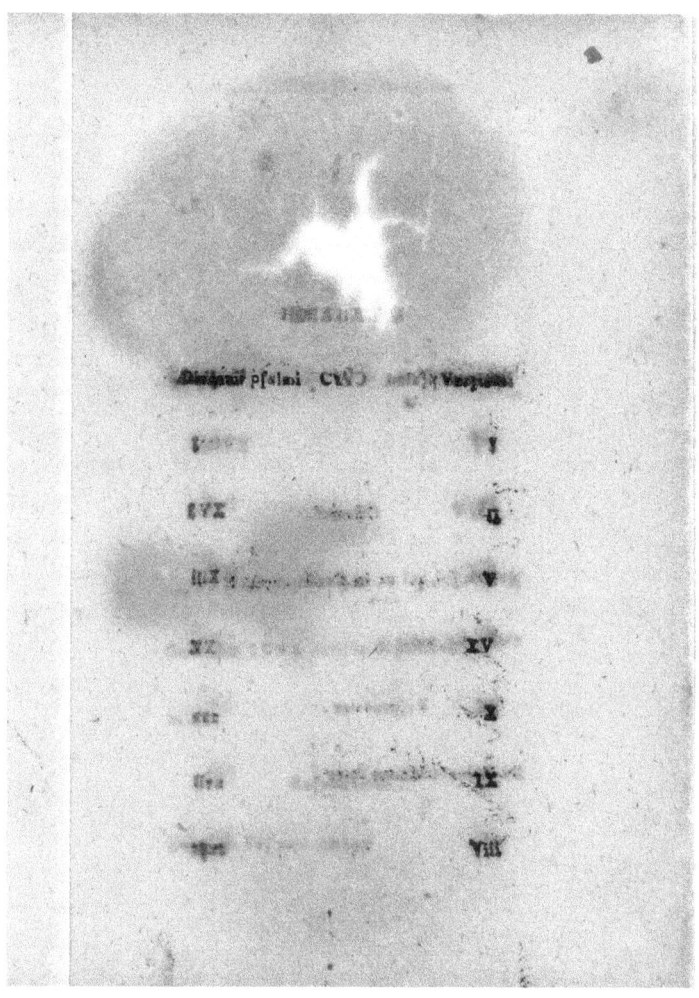

folio 18r.

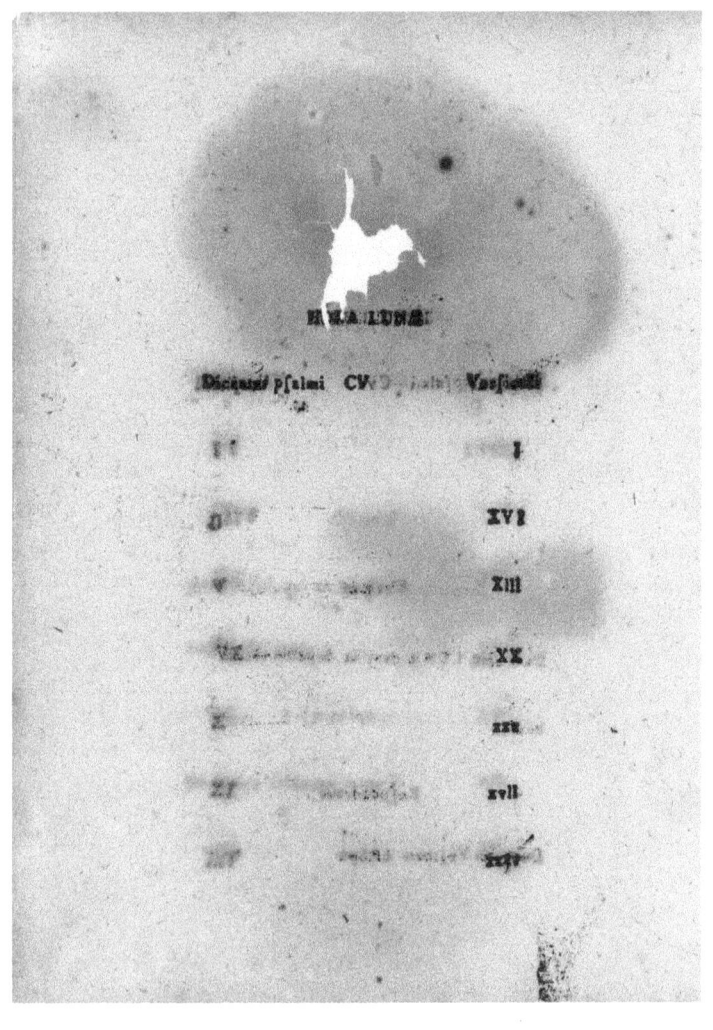

folio 18v.

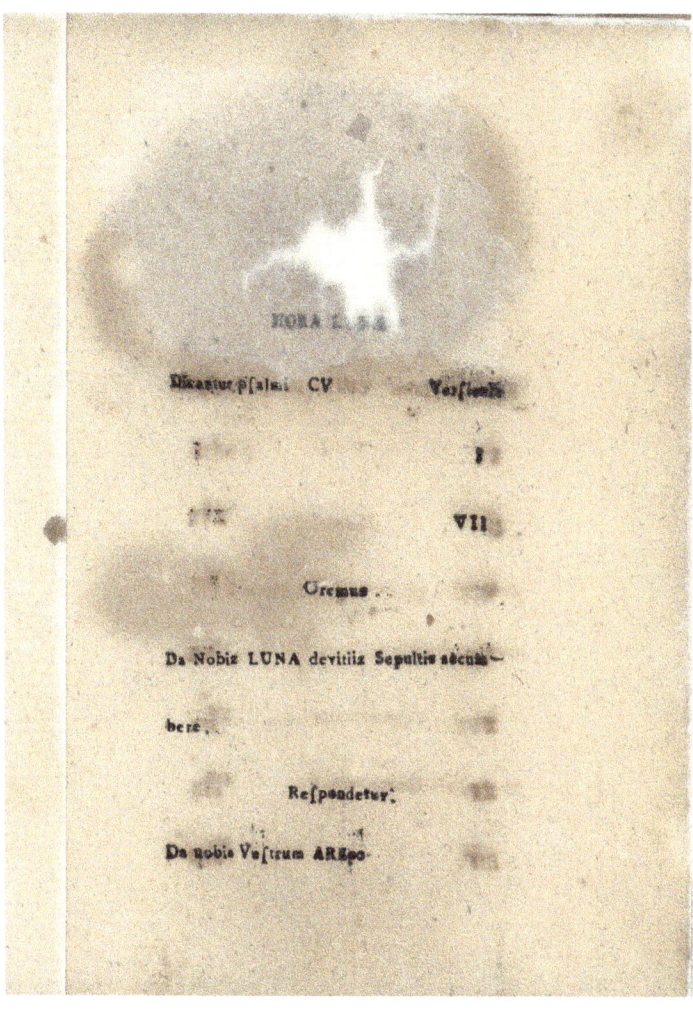

folio 19r.

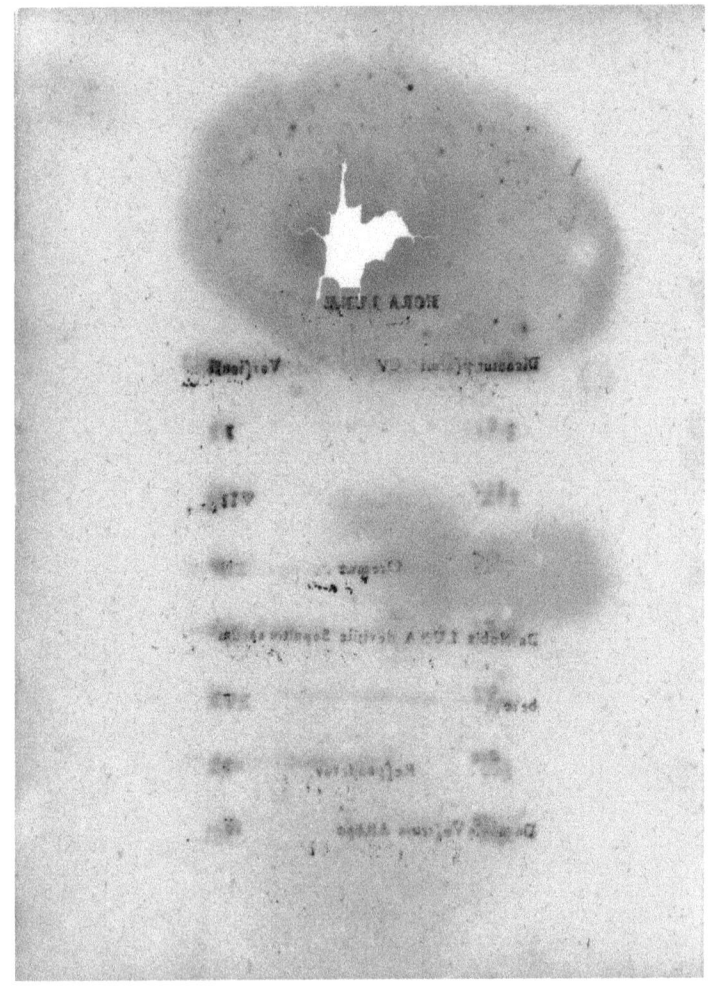

folio 19v.

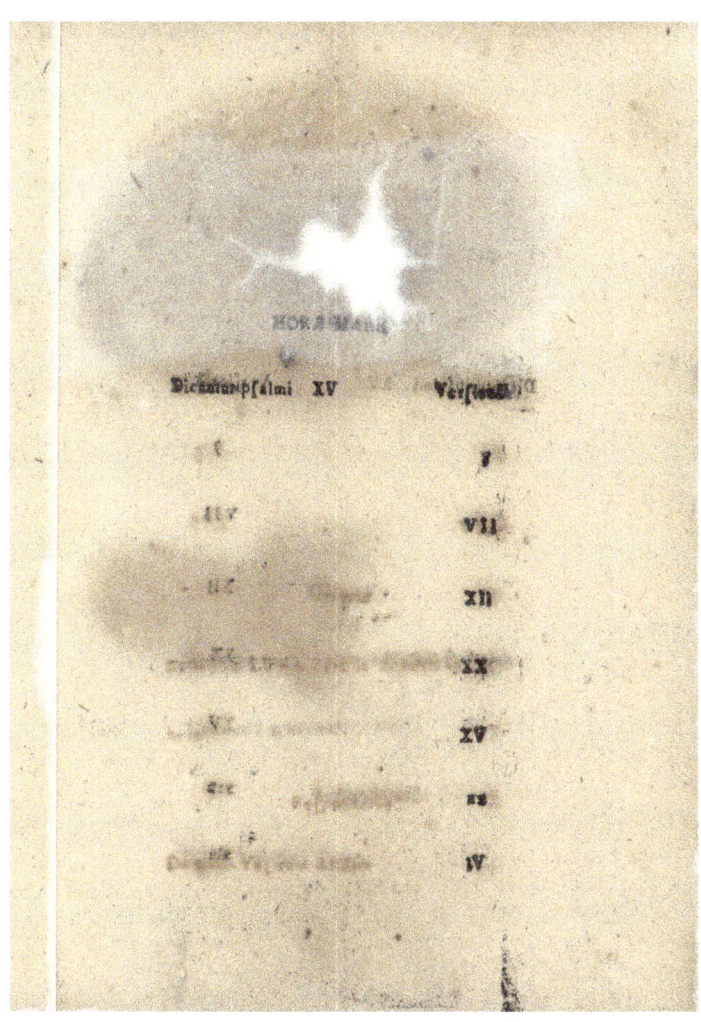

folio 20r.

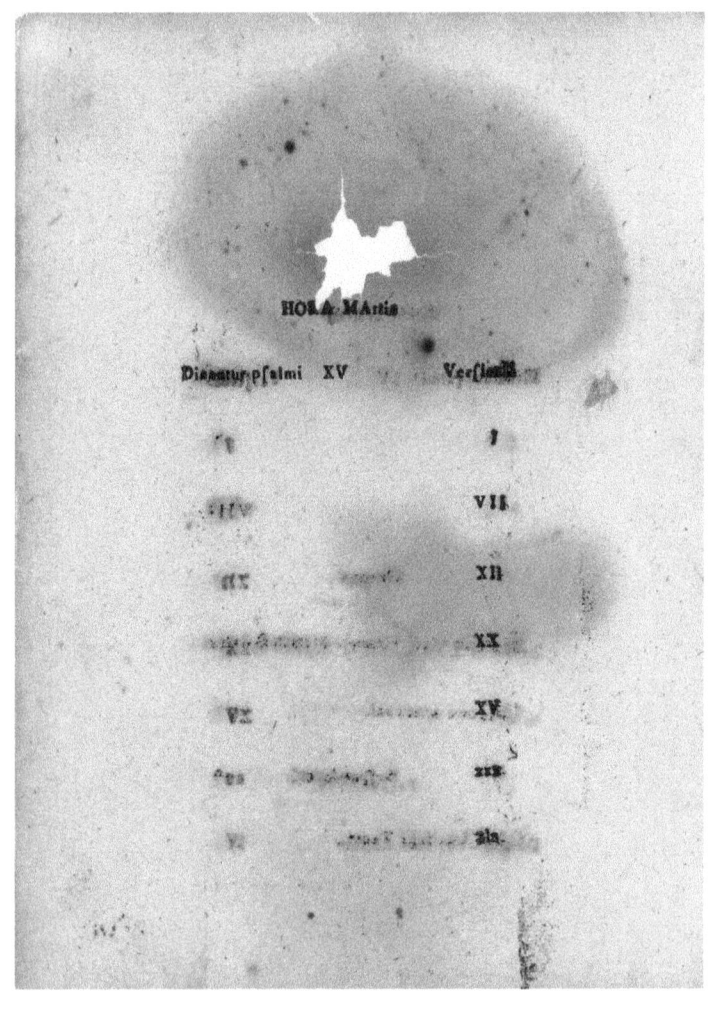

folio 20v.

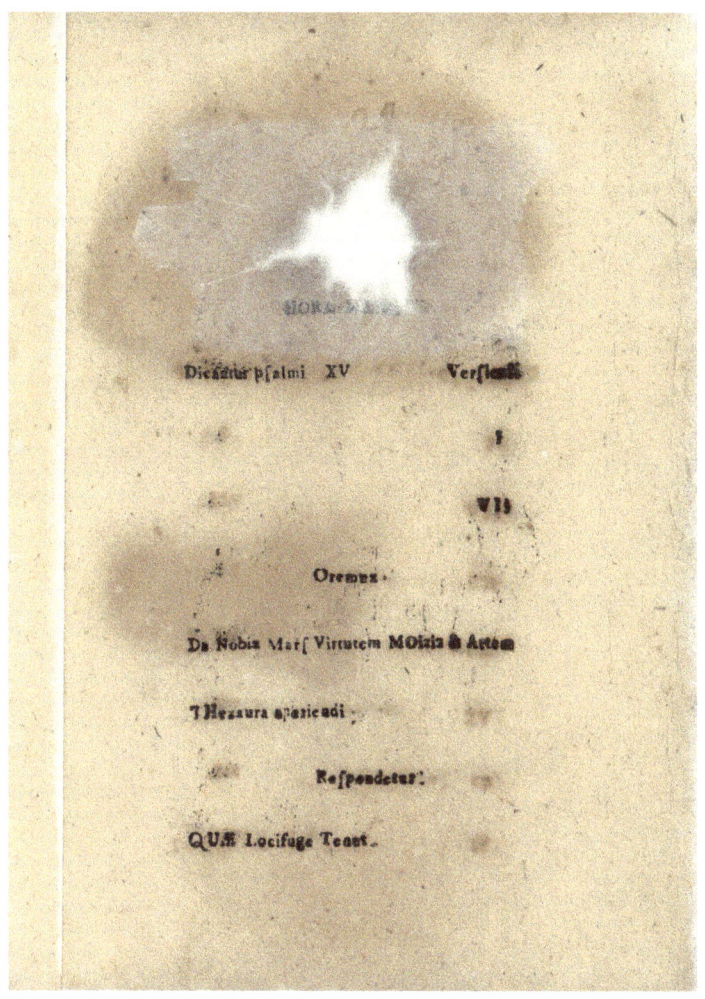

folio 21r.

folio 21v.

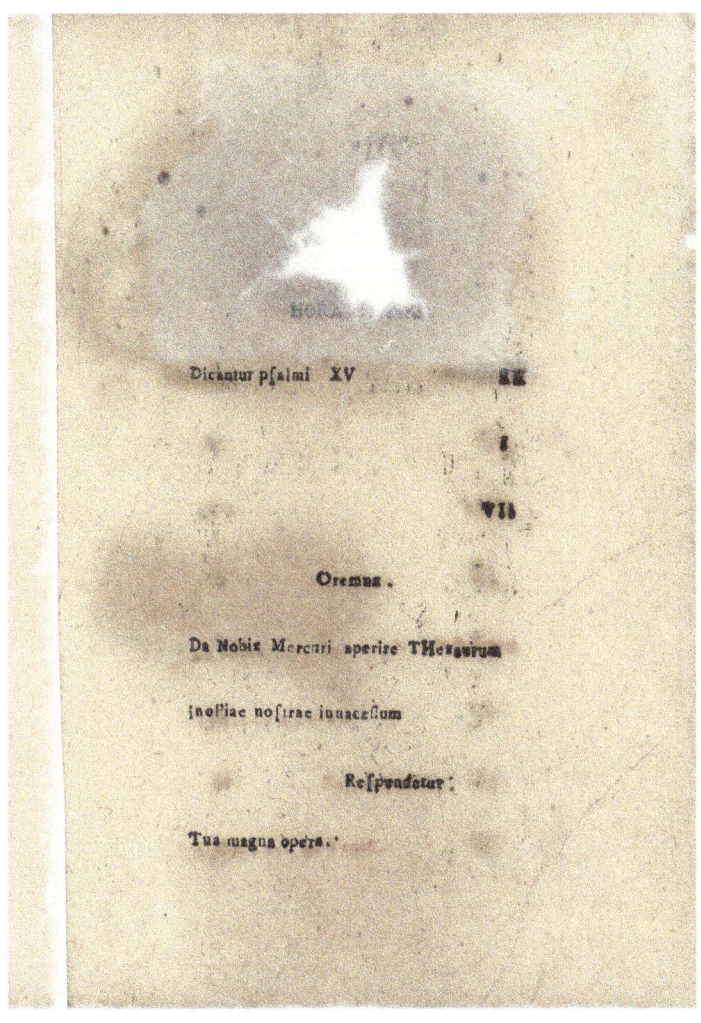

folio 22r.

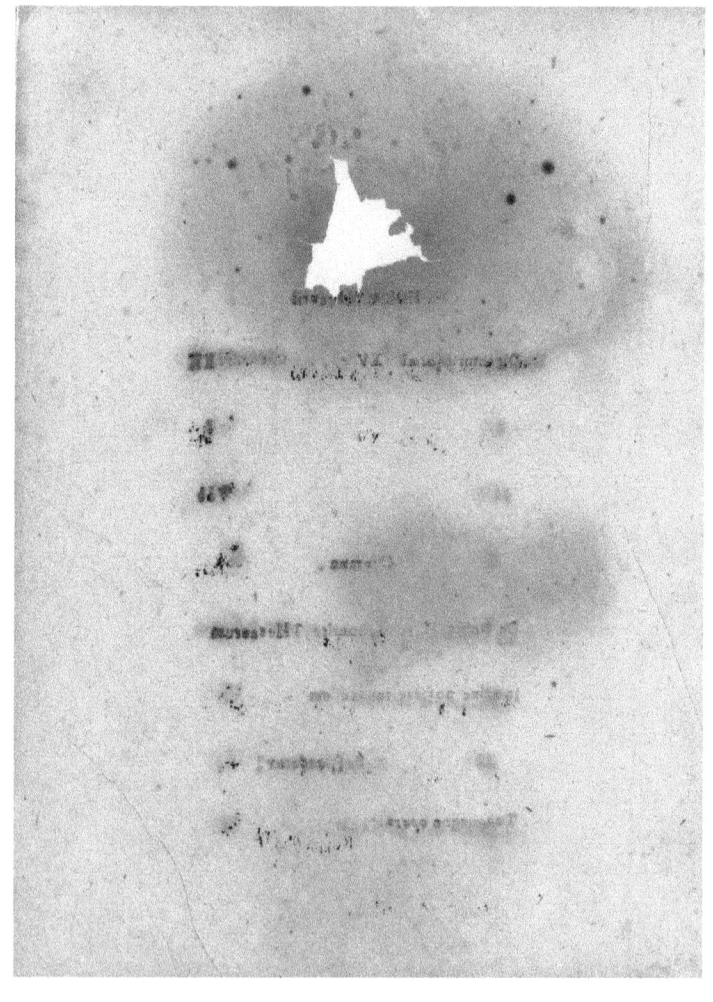

folio 22v.

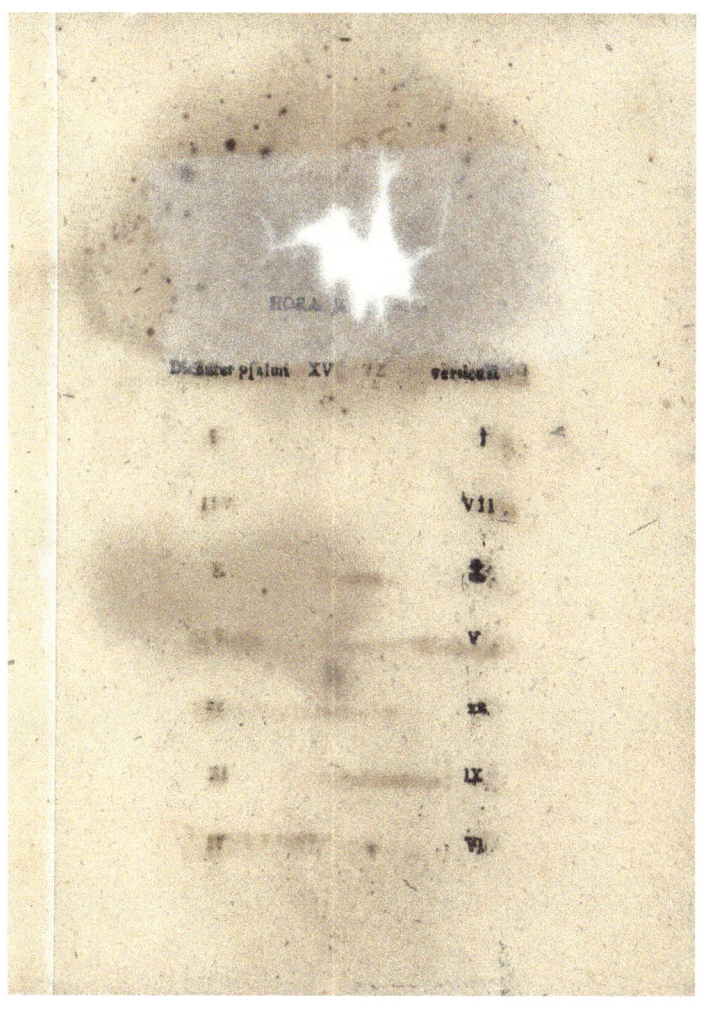

folio 23r.

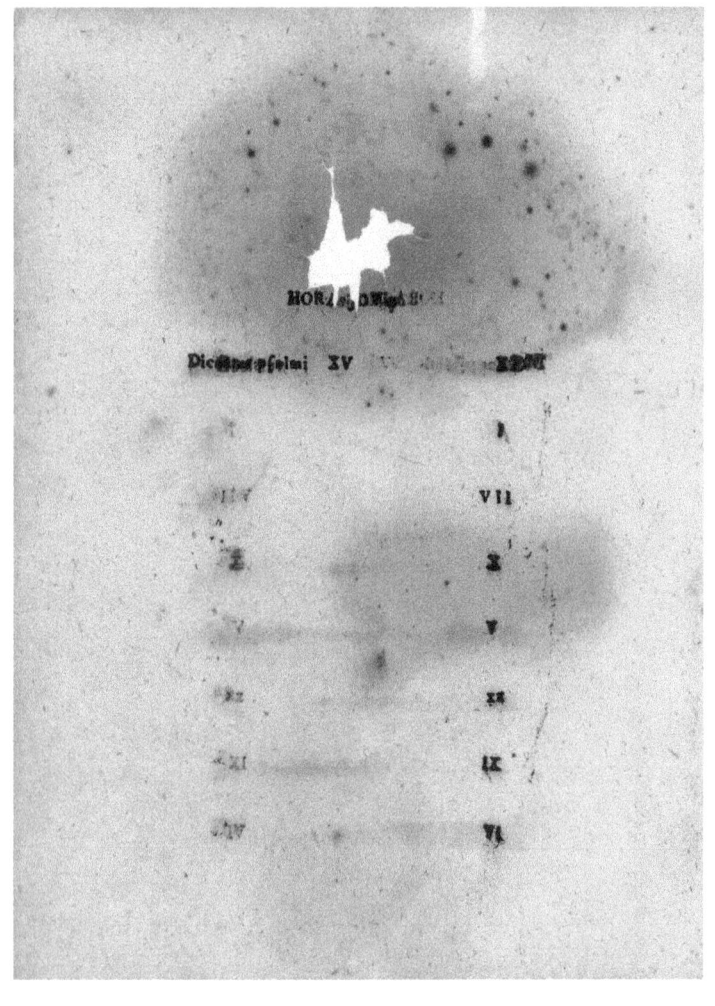

folio 23v.

Cypriani Magici Septem Horae Magicae Facsimile

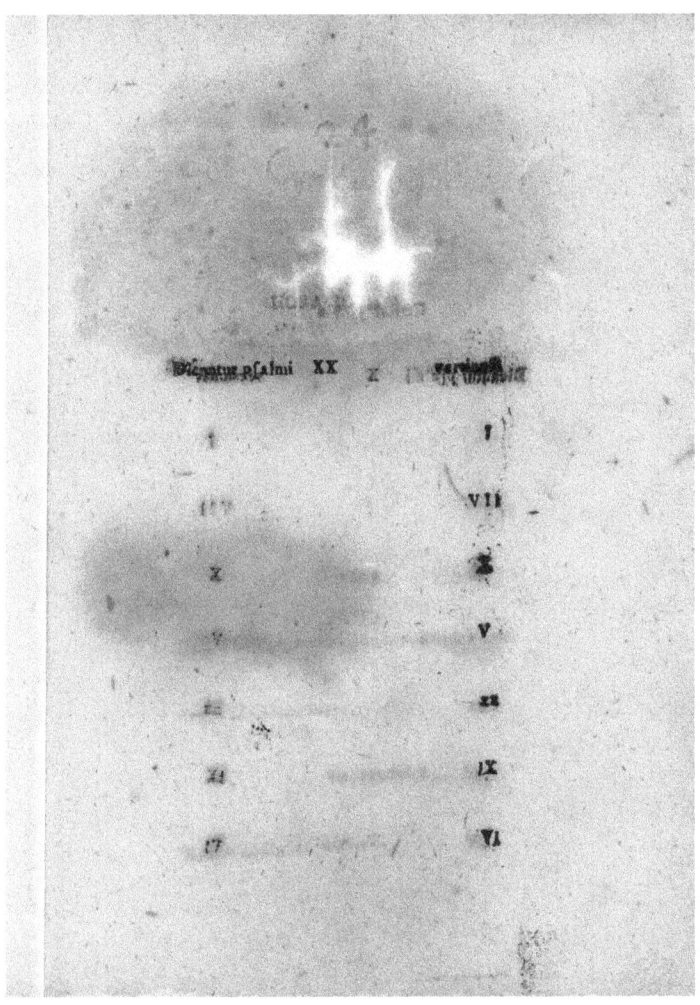

folio 24r.

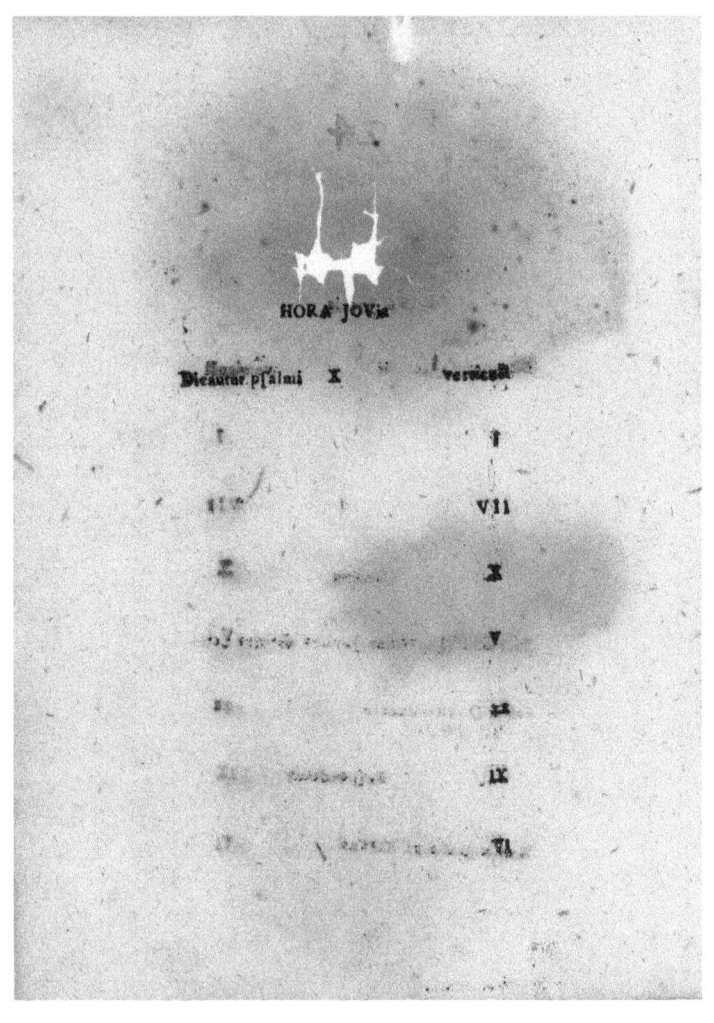

folio 24v.

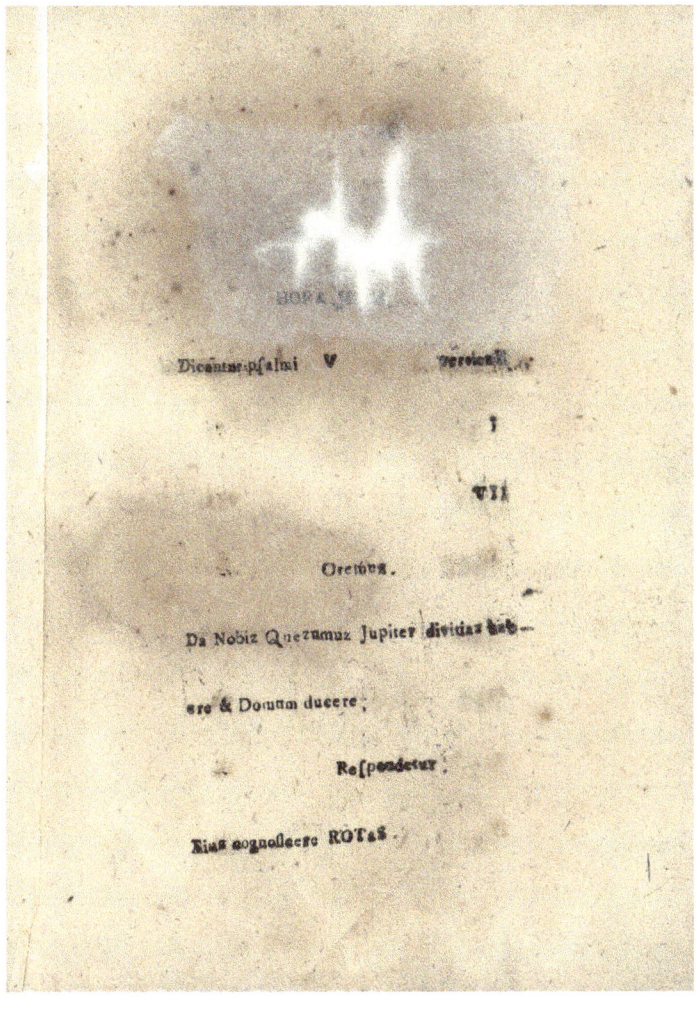

HORA ...

Dicantur psalmi V   versicul...

V

VII

Oremus.

Da Nobis Quæsumus Jupiter divitias hab-

ere & Domum ducere.

Respondetur.

Eius cognoscere ROTAS.

folio 25r.

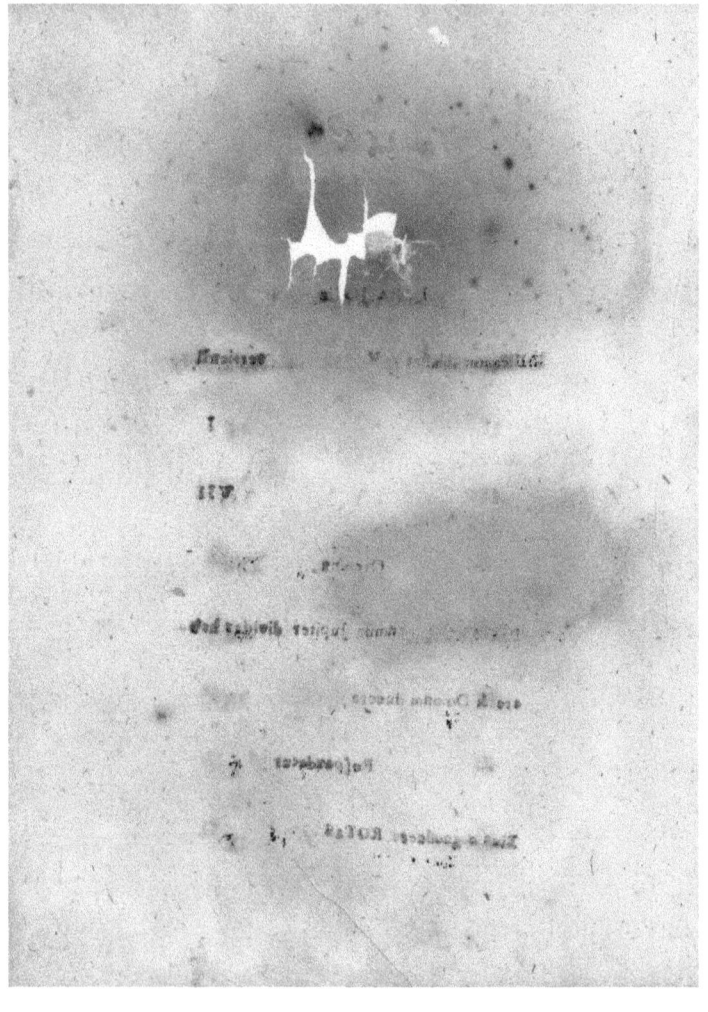

folio 25v.

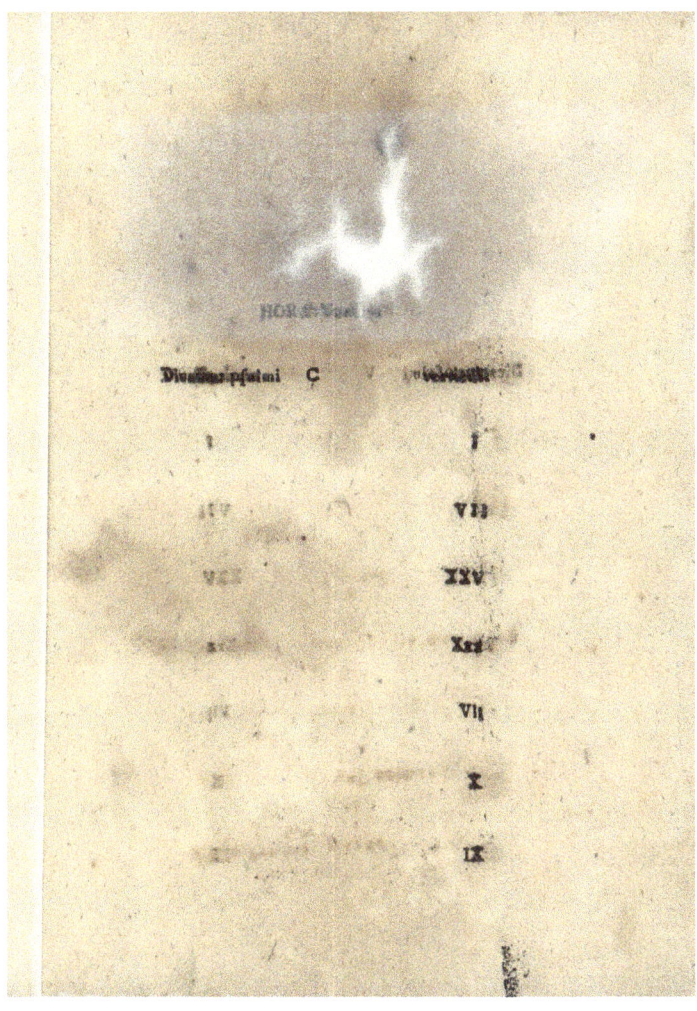

folio 26r.

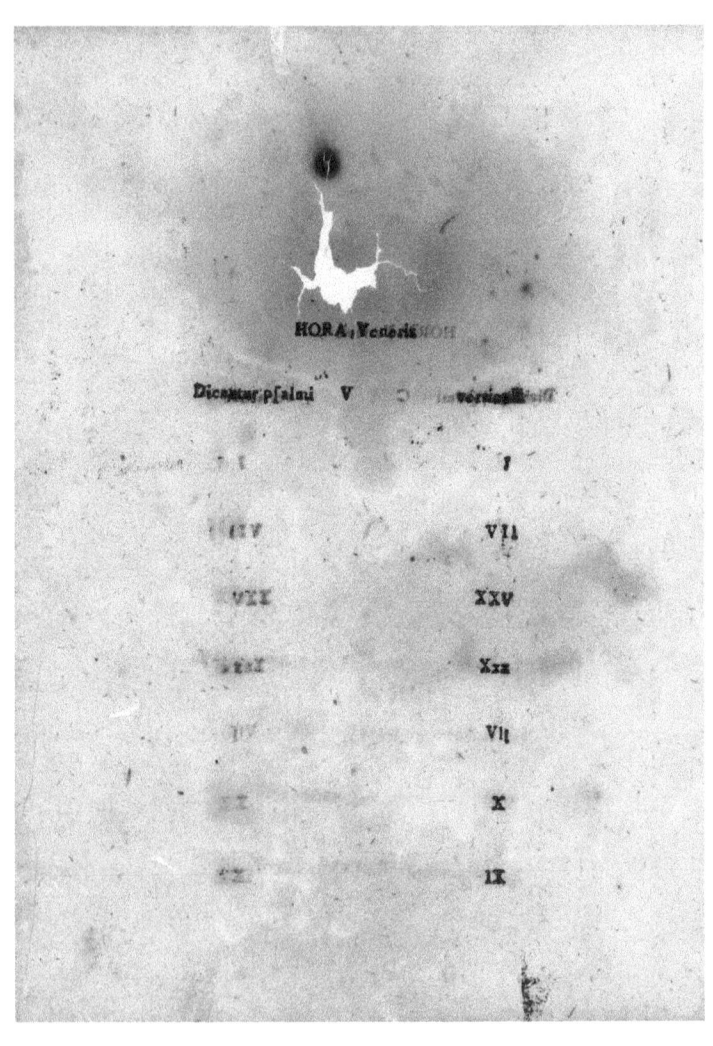

Cypriani Magici Septem Horae Magicae Facsimile

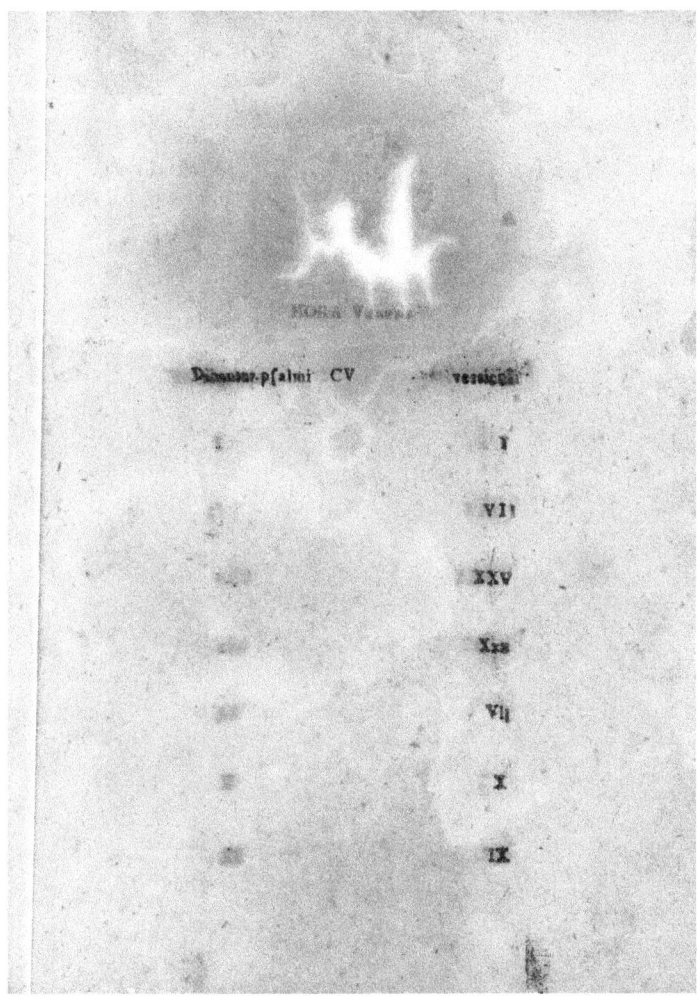

folio 27r.

Cypriani Magici Septem Horae Magicae

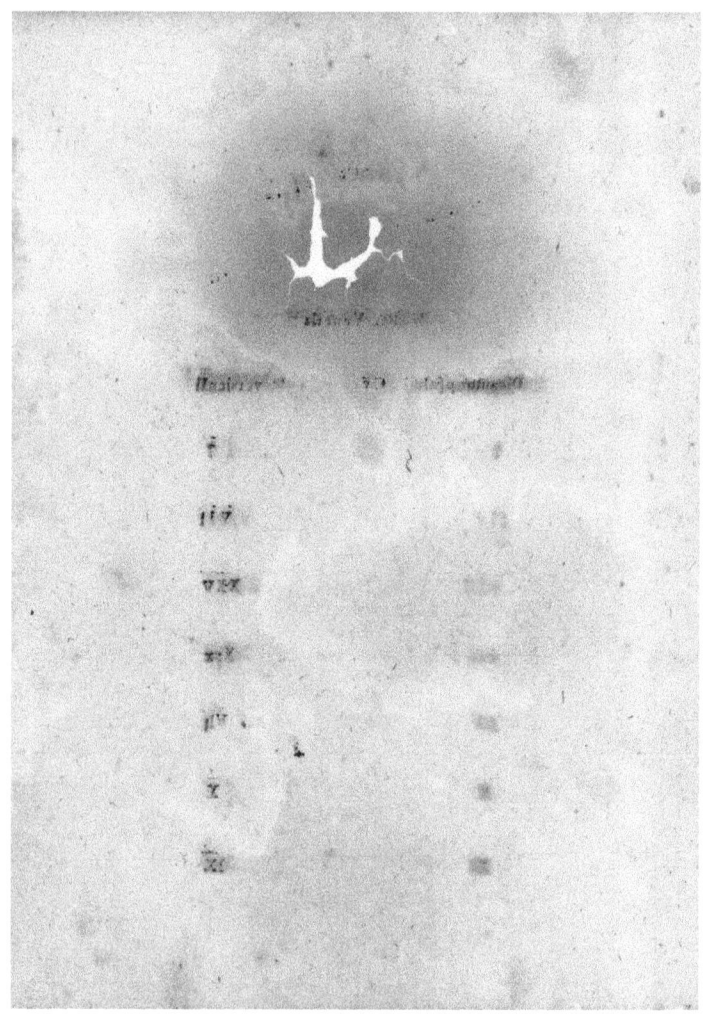

folio 27v.

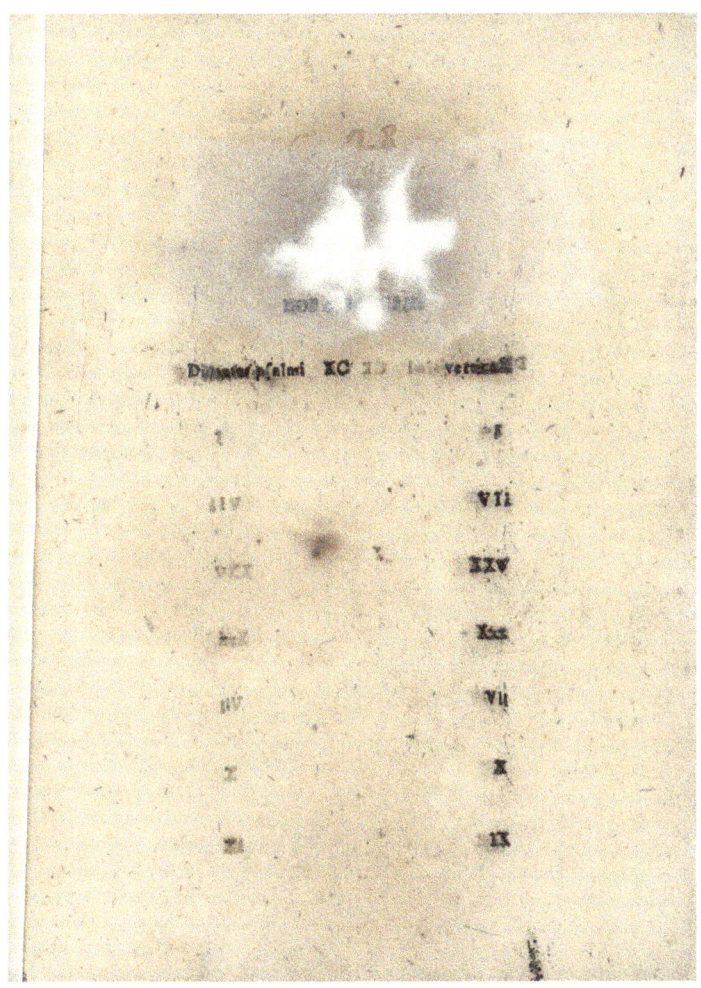

folio 28r.

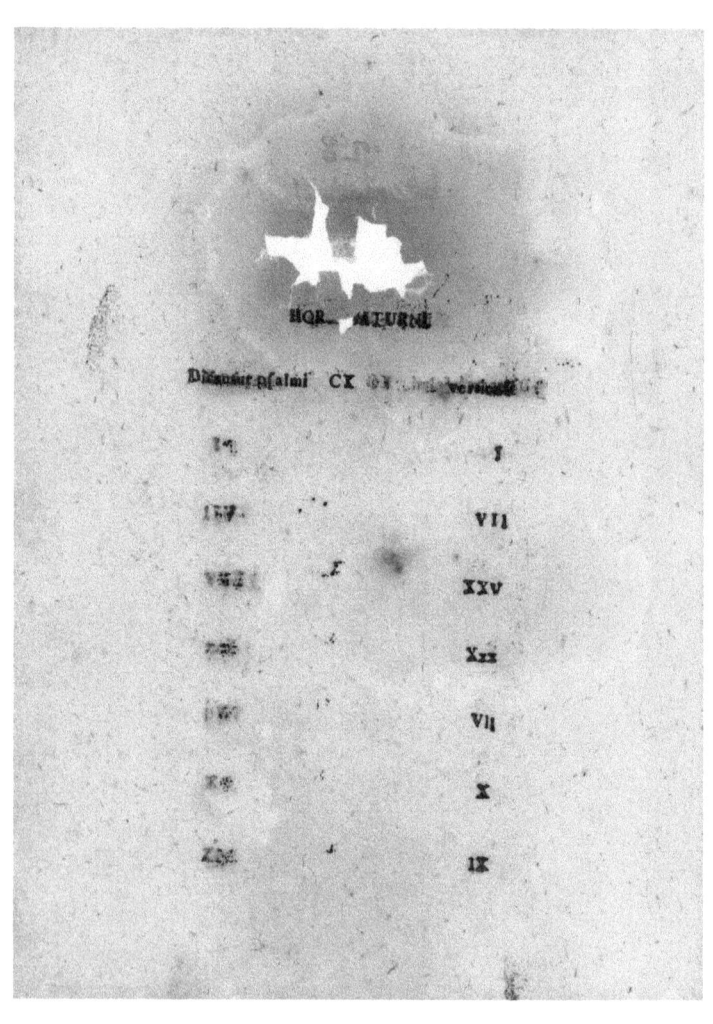

folio 28v.

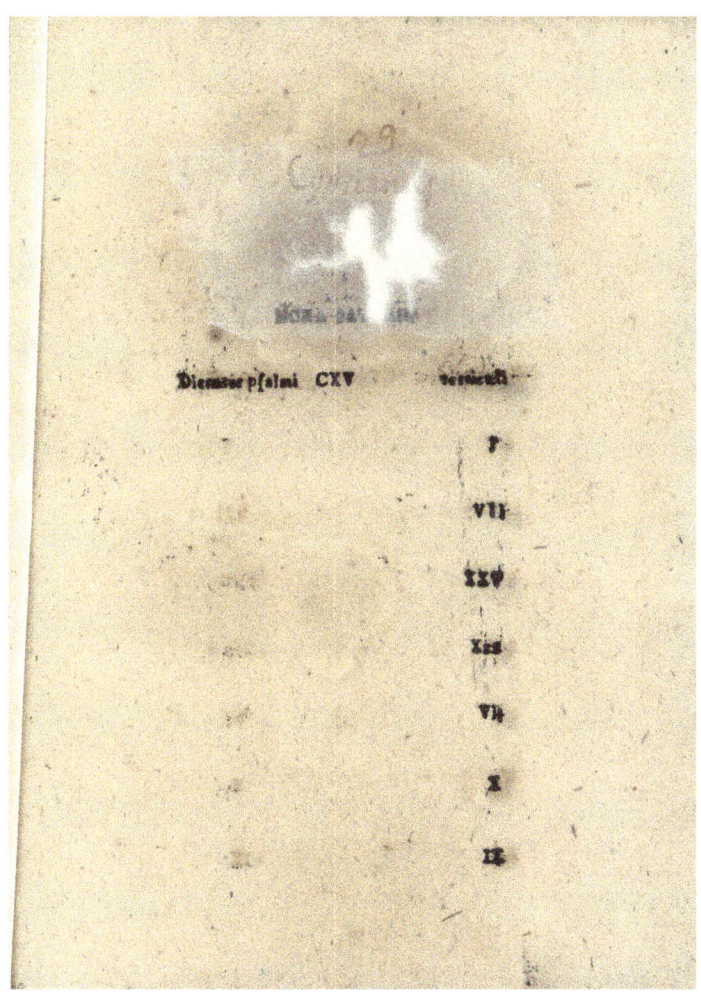

folio 29r.

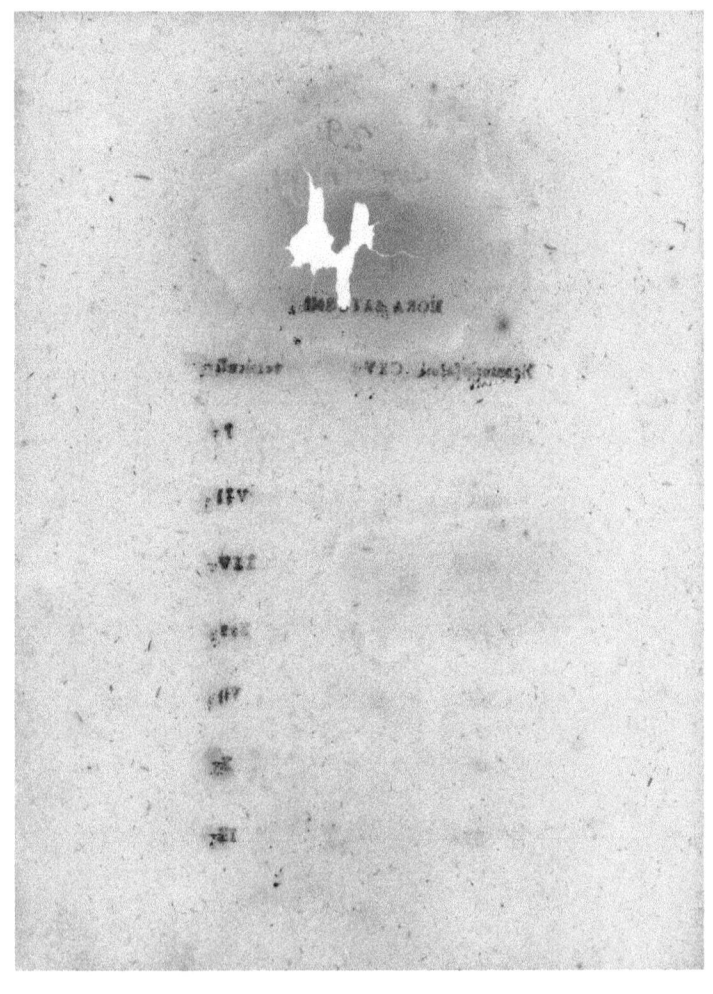

folio 29v.

Cypriani Magici Septem Horae Magicae Facsimile

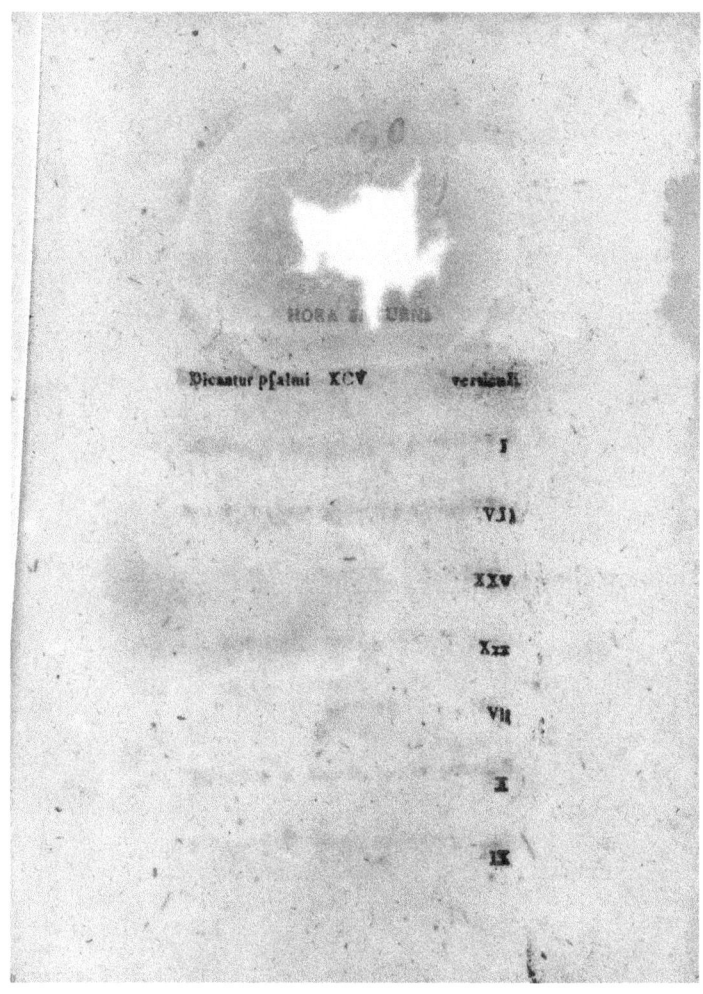

folio 30r.

folio 30v.

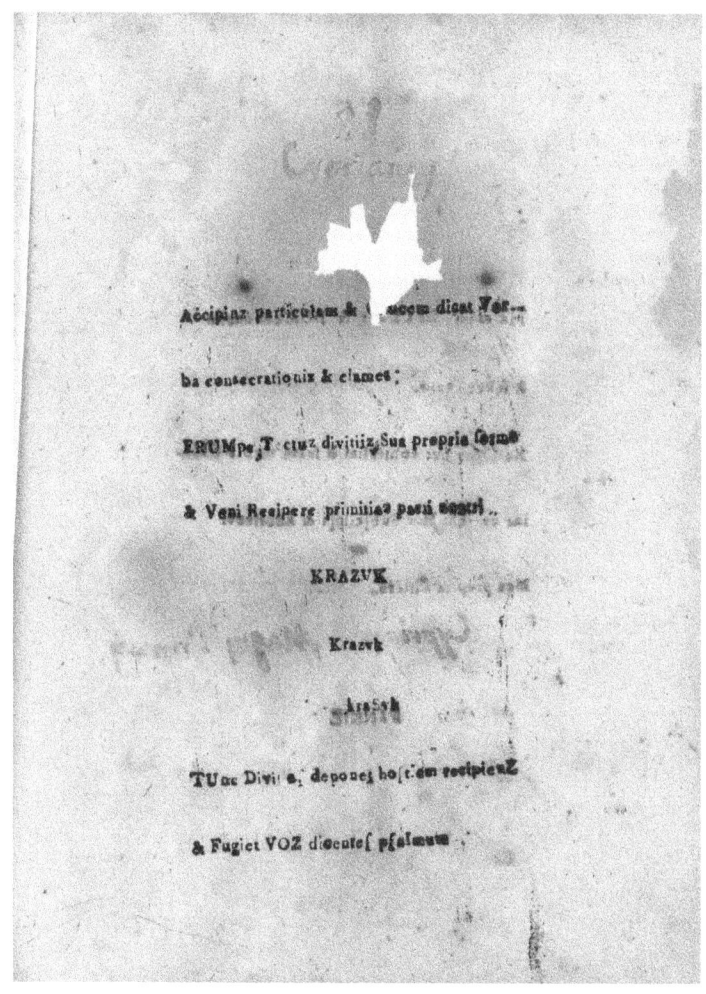

folio 31r.

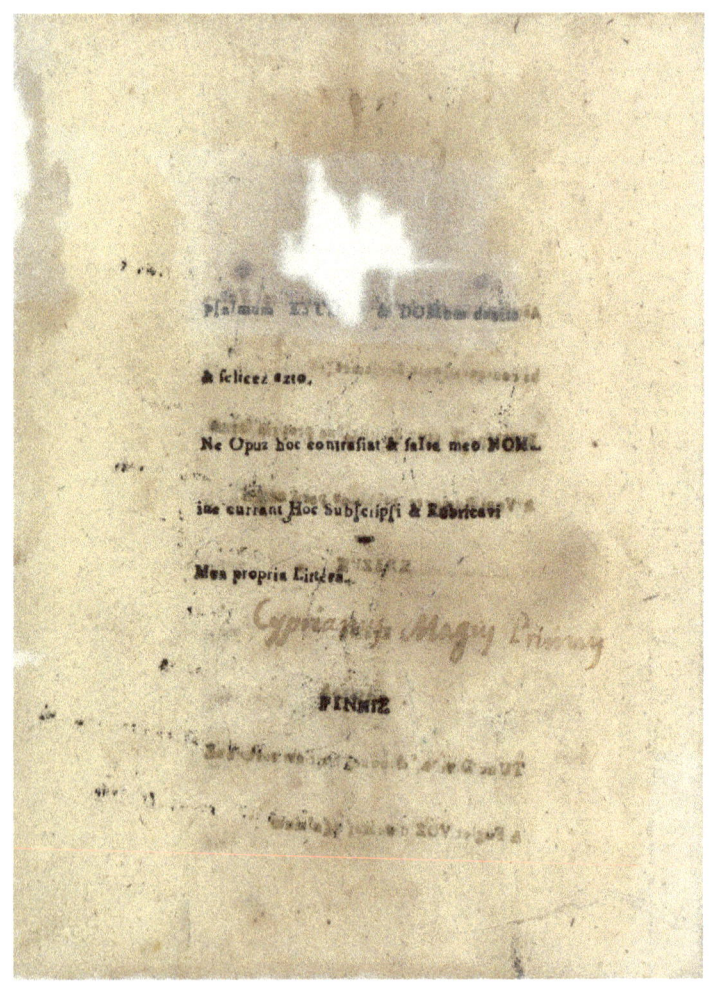

folio 31v.

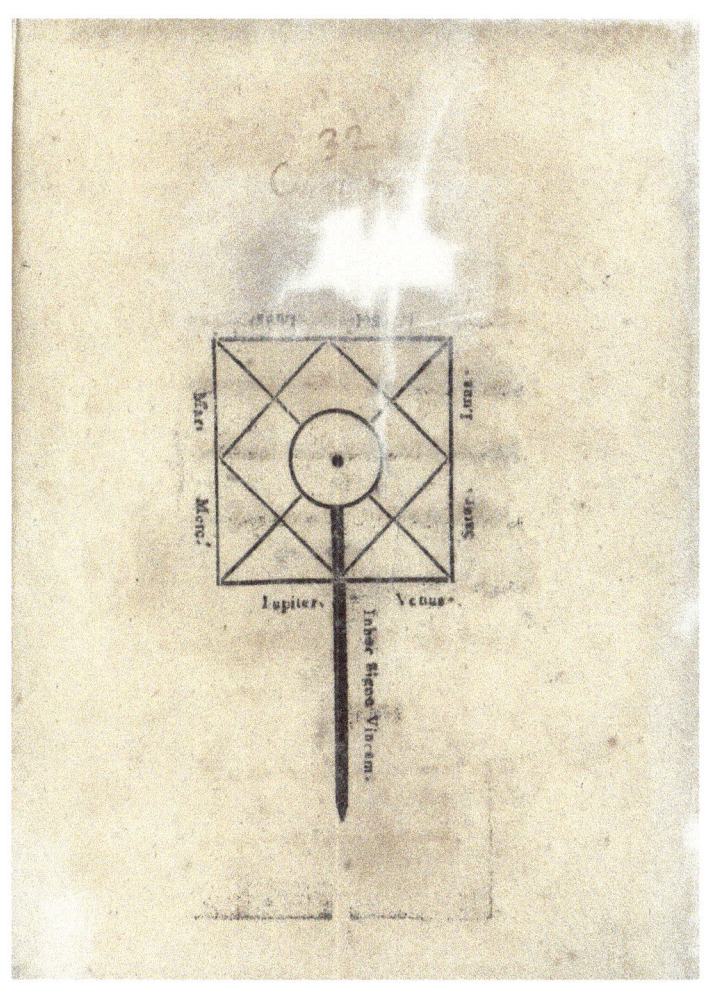

folio 32r.

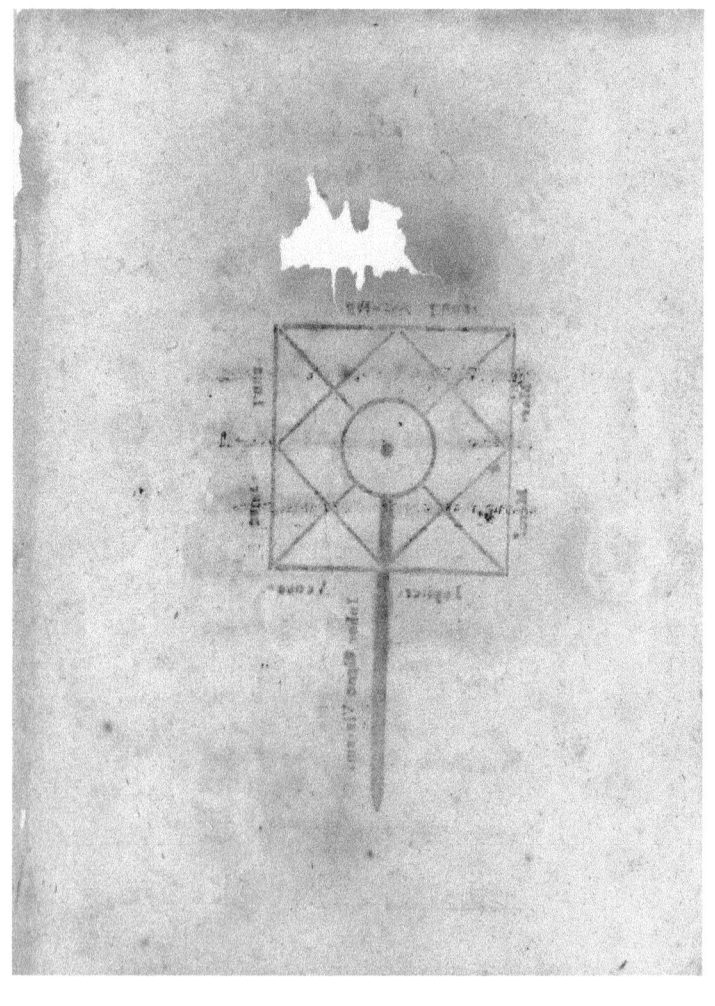

folio 32v.

folio 33r.

folio 33v.

Cypriani Magici Septem Horae Magicae Facsimile

folio 34r.

Cypriani Magici Septem Horae Magicae

Transcription

Key:
{} indicate lacunae or other textual obfuscations caused by physical damage to the book.
<> indicate conjectural readings of uncertain passages, interpolations for clarity, or words left untranslated due to illegible text.

CYPR{I}ANI {MAG}ICI

SEPTEM {H}ORÆ

Magicae

Cyprianus

Editae ab ipso Bernae

anno

154{...}

Cyprianus[123] gratia {...}th[124] Locifuge Refocele et eiusdam omnium potestatum Universi Magust[125] primust, cui tantunmodo[126] cognosscere Magiae arcana principalia, et solere de sinu Terrae unica et generali methodo Thesaura omnia invenire

---

123 Fol.2r.

124 In the Adolfo Coelho transcript, this 'th' seems to have been visible as 'buth', which he assumes refers to 'Belsebuth'. We are currently unable to confirm or deny this reading.

125 The text frequently uses what appears to be an 'st' ligature where standard orthography would have an 's'; this has been preserved in the transcription.

126 Likewise, 'n' often takes the place of 'm'. Irregular spellings—to say nothing of inverted letters—are common throughout the text; the most frequently-occurring examples will be noted at the first instance of each, others included without comment.

concessum fuit, nunc pro viribus meis atenuatiz[127]
Magicandi <...>, et parvulos {in}opiam suam perdere
{volens ... ... argentum omne}[128] et aurum, sicut alia pretioza
in terra iam dudum Magiae virtute detenta: has septem
horaz Magicaz eidem didico sequentibuz notiz, primo:
De antiquiz Solum: ADAMI MAEGIE, quae vera est De
paradiso omni Boni ac MaLI Cientia expulsus est.

SECUNDO: N{emo} Thesaura haurire de{siderans ... FI}
CAN[129] quaerat MULIeRes, i{st}ae raro pactum suficiens
habend:Quaerite egonum Vel CLeRICUN, qui pro interia
LoCifUGe THeZAurorun custode pactun faciat, et FiDe

Legat vel a sacerdote audienZ pronuncied[130] omnia infra
scriPta.

    MAGiAE artez abjudicate manu, quia in illiz
aliquid deficiet, et tantum mea propria[131] manu subsc{ripta,
et Typis edita} Valend, ed solum in ips{is datet} <Potente>
pactum Verun faciendi.

TERTIO: WFTFKeZ[132] INQirite de Locis
ab MAUriz oliu Possessiz, et investigate notantes scopulos
omnes, signa aliqua habentes, huiusmodi ab illiz ad posite a
obtinenda Loca pozita sacere, quia {... ... ...} credeba{t}[133]

---

127 'z' for 's'.

128 Fol.2v.

129 Fol.3r.

130 'd' for 't'.

131 Fol.3v.

132 Sic; this seems to be nothing more than an artifact of the printing process with no grammatical place in the text.

133 Fol.4r

QUARto: Assero, omnibus Horis tribus cuiusque diei praeste unumquemque plane tarun: ITA TRibuz primiz Posd ortun soliz praest sol: sequentibuz Luna: aliiz Mars: aLiiZ: Mercuriusi: postea IUpiter: deinde VENUZ ac saturnus ultimiS Luna, et[134] sic de{... ...} MAURI THezaura arte MAGiae servasund, ea ssacrando planetae in hora incantacioniz dominanti: ed aliis ordine quo indicantur in septem TELARibuz Magiae, et ipsio ordine Horae Magicae recirandae Se ad.

Magiae Telarium Conztrutio sit method sequendi: IN {Caniculae} DIe, horis[135] saturni, insru{...} fieri CUpresti materian coligite, & Rociiz noctiz Regum MAGoram Subiicite per Tempuz Ioviz & VENERiZ: De ila Virgas quatuor parate ad quinquginta policez extencax & cuius periferia policem & dimidiam habead:
ILLIZ QUADratum ed angulos iungite de uribz Laniaribuz LUpi Masculi, interfecti horis LunaE IULLii[136] crecente, p{...}uz quam alio Tempore, quia eo faciliuz concervantur absqui Tenie. Eoden Modo Cinamo nun habere, & cuiusque ALTariz Latere MIssam habente in eodem die ponite CUN ilo parate ToD ViRGaZ extensas, ita ud Longe Habeantur per policez, quod ab medio ad mediun UNIUscuiustque lateriz ALTERius Quadrati aplicari valeant Alium[137] QUADRA{TU}M HIZ Facite, iungendo anguloz azini dentibuz Laniaribuz. QUadratun hok iLo iungite, anguliz interni medio LaTERUN eXTeRNi rezpondentibuz. De anguLiZ HUius ad LaTerum ilius MeDium Virgas quatuor Fagi fixate & UNaQuaque parte EXTerni midia scribite

---
134 Fol.4v.
135 Fol.5r.
136 Fol.5v.
137 Fol.6r.

sequentia sol, Luna, Mars, Mercurius, Iupiter, Venus, Saturnus, & luna.

DE[138] QUATU{...}LIS Quadrati {...}<...> ad eius centrum VIRGAZ Roboris eodem modo secty Protendite modo <...> iungantur in annulo, furamen duarum policum postidente. EoDeM MoDo sex allia Quadrata parate: Deinde Horiz IoViZ in die MaGorum Virgam olivae recipe longaM ad XXXXVii polices <...> Nigri in CoNUbiorum Tempore occisii, ocisi[139] CApUT FIXA{R}E VIRGae MEDIo, inde ad apicem aequalibus distantiaz Vii

QUadrate Magiae figite, subiectiz unicuique duobuz sculeiz ferri uti circunvolvantur Lini Maurizci fila ab una Maria, quae habeat annoz XXXXxxxvii, filioz V celibata, in die Magorum facta habeto & <...> CHordam TRium pedum facite, cuius <...> Maerulae Nigrae horis solis.

CAput[140] occizae {...} vinciatur posito cezura oculo FELIZ NIGRI: CHordae extremum aliud apice Virgae vincito & scribite eiuz Longitudine sequentia   IN HOC SICNo ViNcAM: Recipite sulfuris rezinae & BRioniae UNcias V, oLei & cerae Apium Libras iV, iungite Die Magorum et caedetem facite <...> filamento dicto.

De[141] pactu{m} {...}chrando

NoCTE, Hora Ioviz propre FLUMeniz pelagum egenuz aculeo circulum scribad, cuiuz diameter habeat XXXXXxxii

---

138 Fol.6v.
139 Fol.7r
140 Fol.7v.
141 Fol.8r.

policez & SALomoniz simbolum intra fiat IN ANGULiZ accendantur tot Candelae sacrae modo sequenti Recipite UNCTI Humani, pulveriz cranei Defuncti & siulfuris uncias xx

ADEpiz[142] Raiaz Uncias	VII
spermae Ceti	CXX
Ursti Uncti	X
Cerae Novae	cxxxxxx
Adepiz Lupi	V
colubriz uncti	Xii
Moschi	ii
Acafetidae	V

Iungat & Homo pacti fundat foco cedri &[143] Mirii Natalis die {h}ora Ioviz colecti Candelaz V intra simbulum faciat: Deinde LUMine Novo accendat candelaz simboli anguliz: Recipite

oLEI Lampadiz UNcias	II
chordae Sparti	V
Felis Osiium	iV

iungat & UNGenz CAput, Narez, oculos, Manus & AUReZ ostcuLans deinde angula Simboli[144] side pa{... ...}ndi intra <......> incipiat proffetionem:

---

142 Fol.8v.

143 Fol.9r.

144 Fol.9v.

EGO N   CRedo in omnibus suae Horiz Magiciz continentur & Locifuge & influxu planetarum   Reiicio constitucionez in Magiam   ADamuM, Noemun, Salomonun, Daviden & trez Regez veros Magoz este & Telares Magiae necestarioz Operibus Meia.

NO{TA}:[145]

DIE Magorum stolam & Corporalia furtim obtinete & Homo hiis tegad capud &

<...> induad.

Si Legere, Legad & scribad cLericoz et ipce ayat.

Teneo[146] corpor{... ...} ARGUMenta prima Pacti hic facti.

Me pactum hoc Servandun astero si ea LOcifuge mihi Serviaz eo Tempore, quod
signo per haz candelas et Simbolum

   Recipe TantuM, o LUcifuge cuztoz THezaurorun per haz Veztez

NO{TA:}[147]

HIC Ferit digitum minimun Seniztram & <...> Valerianae silveZtris clericust si

ile nesciat scribad, dunmodo HOMo pacti pronuncied & signed sequentia.

---

145 Fol.10r.
146 Fol.10v.
147 Fol.11r.

Unc[148] per Sa{...} & calamum MAGIAE SAcratun Locifuge
Mihi apareat, quotiez prope Thezaurun VERba ista
pronuntiabo:
       cravek

       crasvek

       crassvek

& si bieniun Mortuuz ero ili conmito animan mean quod
nunc tibi EGo N &c..

NOTA:[149]

Hinc scriptum saxo ligatum ad Pelagum dimitid & posd
TRIDUUM eoden Loco & hora cingat stolam et Dictas.

LIGAMen[150] Per hoc, die Magorum Regum ECeleziAE
furtim receptum, LOcifuge tibi Me Lige.

Telarez[151] centro figat {...} primam candelam apice eorum
acendenz et moveaz eoz dicat.

Sic[152] Rota {... ...} {volveret} et quotiez super Thezaurum
Movebitur indicet, quo ordine Horae Magiae Recitandae
sunt.

Deinde[153] Hoztiam ac part{icu}las calice vitreo accipienz
dicat: suzcipe Locifuge primitiaz pacti mei in Memorian

---
148 Fol.11v.
149 Fol.12r.
150 Fol.12v.
151 Fol.13r.
152 Fol.13v.
153 Fol.14r.

Pacti Adami &c.   Deinde Hoztiam levanS dicet:
Hostia Maga da mihi Virtutem Thezaua INVENiendi
Deinde hozTian constumat ParticulaZ

Servet & Recipiat.

ALGaliae et Moski UNCIAs   V

iungat[154] & {... ... ...} & fumi subiiciat Bibliam unam,
per horam dimidiam, qua Recitabit psalmoz a fine ad
initiaz, MUTando Dei &c in Planetae Horae NoMen
QUUM deinde Libebit Loco THEZAURI Simbolun et
Circulun more pacti facite et centro Focum More sequenti
quo extincto candelaz accendad et centro figat TELARez
Magiae.

Recipiat:[155]

Sulphuriz et Mozchi UNCIAZ   Viii

Ostium Defuncti   cxxv

Cupresti & cedri die

Magorum noctu colecti   cxxxxxx

Focum faciat & Sedeant periferia Deinde capud Merulae
movenz Telarez dimitat ab alto & iPsum intranz ostendet,
quo ordine Horae Recitandae sunt VESTez accipiat
CALICEM[156] Vitr{eo} {...} super Telerez ponat, subiecto
uno corporali et per Bibliam dictam pronuntiet Horaz postea
Scriptaz clare & devote.

Oportet HOMINem pacti habere Senistra accencam
candelam primam & capite Lupi pelem.

---

154 Fol.14v.
155 Fol.15r.
156 Fol.15v.

HOR{A}[157] SOL{IS}

Dicantur psalmi	I	
	II	III
	iV	V
	Vii	iX
		XX
		Xix
		Xxvi
		LX

{HORA}[158] SO{LI}S

Dicantur psalmi	LXII
	LXV
	LXIX
	CI
	CV
	XXX
	LV
	xxI

---

157 Fol.16r.

158 Fol.16v.

HORA[159] {SOLIS}

Dicantur psalmi   LXII
VII
VI
Xiii
XVii
XV
C
x{...}

HO{R}A[160] SOLIS

Dicantur psalmi   LXII
XVIII

ORemus:

Nozter sol, qui ez in Cceliz, aurum & argentum da nobis.

Respondetur:

Da Nobiz OMnium Sator.

---

159 Fol.17r.
160 Fol.17v.

HORA[161] LU{NAE}

Dicantur psalmi CV   Versiculi

                                                 I

                                                 II

                                                 V

                                                 XV

                                                 X

                                                 IX

                                                 viii

HORA[162] LUNAE

Dicantur psalmi CV   Versiculi

                                                 I

                                                 XVI

                                                 XIII

                                                 XX

                                                 xxx

                                                 xvII

                                                 xxxv

---

161 Fol.18r.

162 Fol.18v.

HORA[163] LUNAE

Dicantur psalmi CV   Versiculi
                                                          I
                                                          VII

Oremuz:

Da Nobis LUNA devitiiz Sepultim accumbere.

Respondetur:

Da nobis Vestrum AREpo.

HORA[164] MArtis

Dicantur psalmi XV   Versiculi
                                                         I
                                                         VII
                                                         XII
                                                         XX
                                                         XV
                                                         xx
                                                         IV

---

163 Fol.19r.
164 Fol.20r.

HORA[165] MArtis

Dicantur psalmi XV   Versiculi
                            I
                            VII
                            XII
                            XX
                            XV
                            xxx
                            xix

HORA[166] MArtis

Dicantur psalmi XV   Versiculi
                            I
                            VII

Oremuz:

Da Nobiz Mars Virtutem MOiziz & Artem THezaura aperiendi.

Respondetur:

QUAE Locifuge Tenet.

---

[165] Fol.20v.

[166] Fol.21r.

HORA[167] Mercurii

Dicantur psalmi XV   XX
                                              I
                                              VII

Oremuz:

Da Nobiz Mercuri aperire THezaurum inoPiae nostrae innacestum

Respondetur:

Tua magna opera.

HORA[168] JO{VIS}

Dicantur psalmi XV   versiculi
                                              I
                                              VII
                                              X
                                              V
                                              xx
                                              IX
                                              VI

---

[167] Fol.22r.
[168] Fol.23r.

HORA[169] iOViz

Dicantur psalmi XV

XXII
I
VII
X
V
xx
IX
VI

HORA[170] IO{v}iz

Dicantur psalmi XX

versiculi
I
VII
X
V
xx
IX
VI

---

169 Fol.23v.

170 Fol.24r.

HORA[171] IOViz

Dicantur psalmi X	versiculi
	I
	VII
	X
	V
	xx
	IX
	VI

HORA[172] IO{v}iz

Dicantur psalmi V	versiculi
	I
	VII

Oremus:

Da Nobiz Quezumuz Jupiter divitiaz habere & Domum ducere.

Respondetur:

Eiuz cognostcere ROTaS.

---

171 Fol.24v.
172 Fol.25r

HORA[173] Veneriz

Dicantur psalmi C versiculi

                                      I
                                      VII
                                      XXV
                                      Xxx
                                      VII
                                      X
                                      IX

HORA[174] Veneriz

Dicantur psalmi V versiculi

                                      I
                                      VII
                                      XXV
                                      Xxx
                                      VII
                                      X
                                      IX

---

[173] Fol.26r.

[174] Fol.26v.

HORA[175] Veneriz

Dicantur psalmi CV versiculi
I
VII
XXV
Xxx
VII
X
IX

HORA[176] {SATU}RNI

Dicantur psalmi XC versiculi
I
VII
XXV
Xxx
VII
X
IX

---

175 Fol.27r.
176 Fol.28r.

HORA[177] SATURNI

Dicantur psalmi CX   versiculi

                                                            I
                                                           VII
                                                           XXV
                                                           Xxx
                                                           VII
                                                           X
                                                           IX

HORA[178] SA{TUR}NI

Dicantur psalmi CXV   versiculi

                                                           I
                                                           VII
                                                           XXV
                                                           Xxx
                                                           VII
                                                           X
                                                           IX

---

[177] Fol.28v.

[178] Fol.29r.

HORA[179] SATURNI

Dicantur psalmi XCV   versiculi

                                            I

                                            VII

                                            XXV

                                            Xxx

                                            VII

                                            X

                                            IX

Accipinz[180] particulam & {...}uccm dicat Verba consecrationiz & clamet:

ERUMpe, Tectuz divitiiz, Sua propria forma & Veni Recipere primitiaz <passi> noztri

                               KRAZVK

                               Krazvk

                               kraSvk

TUnc Divitia deponet hostiam recipienZ & Fugiet VOZ dicentes psalmum[181] EYU{...} & D{OMem ...} & felicez ezto.

---

179 Fol.30r.
180 Fol.31r.
181 Fol.31v.

Ne Opuz hoc contra fiat & falsa meo NOMine currant Hoc
Subscripsi & Rubricavi Mea propria Littera.

Cyprianus Magus Primus

FINNIZ

Cypriani Magici Septem Horae Magicae

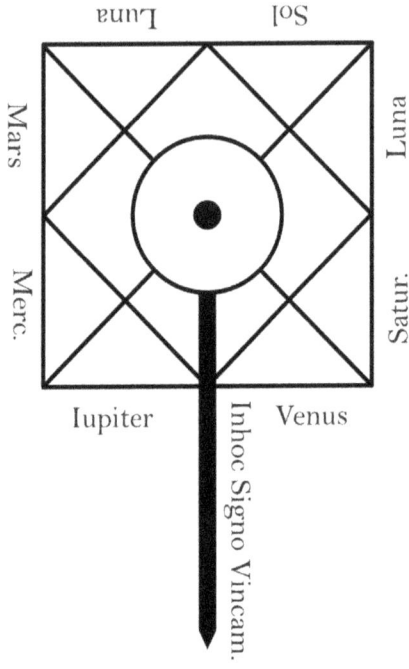

NOTA:[183]

THEZAURUM erit, Caput Merulae intra bit Domos ordine directo vel inverso vel alterno alias non erit vel nunquam esset.

---

182 Fol.32r.
183 Fol.33r.

Cypriani Magici Septem Horae Magicae

Translation

Key:

{} indicate lacunae or other textual obfuscations caused by physical damage to the book.

<> indicate conjectural readings of uncertain passages, interpolations for clarity, or words left untranslated due to illegible text.

[] indicate words or expressions added to the text for 'smoothing' purposes.

The Seven Magical

Hours of

[Cyprian the Mage]

Cyprianus

Published by him at Bern

154{...}

Cyprian[184] thanks {...} Locifuge Refocele[185] and all of his powers. [Regarding] all magic, the <foremost> is simply to know the principal secrets of magic, and to casually discover by particular and general methods every treasure which has been hidden within the hollow of the earth. Now before you weaken my powers <of magic> <.?.>, and youths wishing to eliminate the lack thereof, {... ... all silver}[186] and gold,

---

184 Fol.2r.

185 Besides the clear reference to the spirit Lucifuge Rofocale, there is a possibility that the full name of the spirt being addressed here was 'Belsebuth Locifuge Refocele'

186 Fol.2v.

just as everything precious in the earth has been detained by magical virtue: I proclaim from experience these seven magical hours as follows.

First: From [antiquity, that] the Magic of Adam is true. From paradise [was] all good and evil knowledge [distributed].

Second: {No one} {still wishing ...}[187] to draw up treasures shall pursue women, to whom a pact rarely suffices: And you will need to seek a cleric, who has already[188] made a pact with Locifuge the keeper of treasures, and <he> shall faithfully read [this]; that is, <you shall> hear everything written below recited by a priest.

Abjure magical arts from [your] hand, for something will be lacking in them, insofar as my own[189] hand is able {to write and publish books}, and only by offering these {can} a true pact be made.

Third: Seek the places from which <Moorish olive wood> may be had,[190] and investigate the writings on every <rock/cliff face>, some of them having markings, [in] such places [may] be set a holy location to be obtained,[191] for {... ...} believed.[192]

---

187 Fol.3r.

188 Reading *interim* for *interia* in the text.

189 Fol.3v.

190 Likely a reference to a location of previous Moorish occupation or where these had olive tree groves.

191 Likely an indication that in places found to have ancient carvings on stones (such as in hillforts and ruins) it is proper to establish a ritual space for the enactment of the treasure finding ritual in this book.

192 Fol.4r.

Fourth: I assert that in each hour of every day there stands a <division> representing each one of the planets: So, the first [division] after sunrise represents the Sun: there follow the Moon: then Mars: then Mercury: thereafter Jupiter: next Venus and Saturn <and> finally the Moon, and[193] thus {...} Moorish treasure is <protected> by magical art, sanctified to the planet ruling in the hour of the <enchantment>: and by another <litany> which is indicated in seven magical <talismans>,[194] and one shall recite the magical hours according to that litany.[195]

[The] magical talismans shall be constructed by the following method: During the dog days: in[196] the hour of Saturn, {make ready} to collect <cypress wood>, and on the night <of the Magi Kings> prepare staves in the hours of Jupiter and Venus: Concerning these four staves, make them fifty inches in length and the circumference shall be an inch and a half: Make these into a square and join the corners using the canine teeth from the mouth of a male wolf, killed in the hour of the waxing Moon[197] in July, {...} than in another hour, because they are more easily preserved at that time than otherwise. Now, in the same manner, take cinnamon wood, and each[198] side having been completed in the same day as has been stated, prepare staves long enough that they

---

193 Fol.4v.

194 *TELARibuz*, nom. pl. *telares*; apparently a rare late Latin form, probably derived from Greek *telesma*, 'talisman', possibly influenced by Latin *telare*, 'to weave', from *tela*, 'web', 'loom'.

195 Likely a reference to the psalms prescribed below for the planetary hours.

196 Fol.5r.

197 Fol.5v.

198 Reading *alteris* for *altariz* in the text.

are able to touch consecutive sides of the square from middle to middle and[199] thus make a square, joining the corners with the canine teeth of an ass. This square being joined, the interior corners correspond to the middle of <each> exterior side. From the corners of <the external square> to the middle of each side of <the internal square> affix four beech staves and at the middle of each external part write the sequence Sol, Luna, Mars, Mercurius, Jupiter, Venus, Saturnus, and Luna.

From[200] the {middle of the internal square} to its center you shall extend in the manner {...} staves of oak divided in the same manner, joined to a circle having a hole of two inches. Prepare six other squares in the same way: Then in the hour of Jupiter on the day of the Magi take a stave of olive wood forty seven inches long, a [head of a blackbird] <grafted to it> in the hour it was <decapitated>, affixing[201] the severed head to the middle of the stave, from which <point> affix seven magic squares equidistantly to the end, attaching each one by two iron spikes such that they [may] revolve. On the day of the Magi you shall have threads of Moorish linen made by a [woman named] Maria,[202] who is seventy seven years old, having five celibate sons,[203] and make a <.?.> cord of three threads, of which <.?.> the blackbird in the hours of the Sun.

---

199 Fol.6r.

200 Fol.6v.

201 Fol.7r.

202 Objects owned or produced by women named Maria are a common reference in treasure and *moura* disenchant stories; these are also frequent in certain forms of folk magic.

203 Probably a reference to these being priests.

The[204] severed head {...} shall be bound with an eye cut from a black cat: Fasten the other end of the cord to the end of the stave and write on its length the following: IN HOC SIGNO VINCAM: Take five ounces of sulfur resin and briony, four pounds of beeswax and oil, mix on the day of the Magi and make <the thread> as aforesaid.

Of[205] the {Sacred} Pact

At night, in the hour of Jupiter, near a river by the sea, you will need a spike to inscribe a circle having a diameter of seventy-two inches, and the seal of Solomon shall be made within [this].[206] In the angles shall be lit that many consecrated candles, of a sort as follows:

Take 20 ounces of sulfur, human grease, and pulverized skull of a dead man

the[207] fat of a ray,	7 [oz.]
seed of a whale/shark,	120 [oz.]
bear grease,	10 [oz.]
new wax,	160 [oz.]
wolf fat,	5 [oz.]
snake oil,	12 [oz.]
musk,	2 [oz.]
asafoetida,	5 [oz.]

---

204 Fol.7v.
205 Fol.8r.
206 Likely a pentagram.
207 Fol.8v.

Mix, and one shall spread out the pact by a brazier of cedar, and on[208] the day of the Nativity of Mary in the hour of Jupiter, [with] five candles having been prepared within the seal, light [them] in the angles of the seal with a new taper:

Take lamp oil	2 [oz.]
sprigs of spartum,	5 [oz.]
cat bone,	4 [oz.]

Mix and anoint head, nostrils, eyes, hands, and ears <and lips>. Then in an angle of[209] the seal you shall sit {... ...} inside <.?.> shall begin the profession:

I, N., trust in all that your magical hours hold, and Locifuge, and the influx of the planets. I deny that your magical systems, Adam, Noah, Solomon, David and the Three Kings, are truly magical, and magical talismans are necessary for my work.

Note:[210]

On the day of the Magi you shall keep stole and corporal[211] hidden and one shall thus cover [his] head and don <.?.>.

If <you cannot> read, a cleric may read and write and make the affirmation himself:

---

208 Fol.9r.
209 Fol.9v.
210 Fol.10r.
211 An altar linen used in the performance of mass.

I swear[212] {on this corporal} [that the principal pact is] thus established. I declare this pact has been preserved by me so thereby Locifuge shall serve me at the time at which I indicate by these candles and seal. Accept as much, o Lucifuge, guardian of treasures, by these vestments.

Note:[213]

Here one stabs the left little finger and <.?.> wild valerian <and> a cleric may write [the pact] if you are unable, so long as one recites and signs the pact as follows.

Thus[214] by {...} and consecrated magical pen Locifuge shall appear to me whenever these words are pronounced near treasure:

cravek

crasvek

crassvek

and if I am dead within two years I promise to him my spirit which I, N., now offer to you, etc.

Note:[215]

Then, tying the text to a rock, cast it into the sea, and after three days, at the same place and hour, one shall don the stole and recite:

---

212 Fol.10v.
213 Fol.11r.
214 Fol.11v.
215 Fol.12r.

By[216] this bond, taken secretly in a church on the day of the Magi Kings, Locifuge I bind myself to you.

One[217] shall affix the talismans to the center {...} [light] the first candle, [and] from this you shall light and ignite <the others>, reciting.

Thus[218] the wheel {... ...} {is turned}[219] and whenever it indicates that it has been moved over a treasure, the litany[220] of that magical hour shall be recited.

Then,[221] taking pieces of the host and a glass chalice, recite: Accept, Locifuge, the first fruits of my pact in memory of the pact of Adam etc. Then raise the host, reciting: Magical host, give to me the power to discover treasures. Then one shall consume a piece of the host.

Keep at hand and take:

civet and musk   5 [oz.]

Mix[222] and {... ...} and suffumigate a Bible for a half hour, while reciting the psalms from end to beginning, exchanging God, etc. for the name of the planet of the hour.

---

216 Fol.12v.

217 Fol.13r.

218 Fol.13v.

219 Likely a reference to the moving sections of the 'talisman'.

220 Psalm.

221 Fol.14r.

222 Fol.14v.

Then when one wishes <to know> the place of a treasure, you shall fashion the seal and circle according to the pact, and in the center a brazier in the manner following, from which the extinguished candles shall be lit, and in the center you shall affix the magical talismans.

Take:[223]

sulfur and musk	8 [oz.]
bones of the dead	125 [oz.]
cypress and cedar, collected by night on the day of the Magi,	160 [oz.]

Prepare a brazier and sit next to it. Then, the head of the blackbird being moved, <one shall> cast the talismans down from on high, and it will reveal the entrance,[224] at which point the litany of the hour shall be recited. Take the vestments, the[225] glass chalice {...} place <it> upon the talismans, a <host> being placed under <it>, and as the Bible is read, recite the hours written hereafter clearly and devoutly.

It behooves one who would have a pact to light the leftward candle first, and to skin the wolf's head.[226]

---

223 Fol.15r.

224 This likely means that the earth is supposed to open to reveal a hidden treasure.

225 Fol.15v.

226 Uncertain, but this could be a reference to the source of the wolf teeth needed to secure the several staves of the 'talisman'.

Hour[227] of the Sun

Recite psalms[228] I, II, III, IV, V, VII, IX, XX, XIX, XXVI, LX

Recite[229] psalms LXII, LXV, LXIX, CI, CV, XXX, LV, XXI

Recite[230] psalms LXII, VII, VI, XIII, XVII, XV, C, XC[231]

Recite[232] psalms LXII, XVIII

Prayer: Our Sun, who art in heaven, give to us gold and silver.

Response: Give to us, progenitor of all.

Hour[233] of the Moon

Recite psalm CV, versicles I, II, V, XV, X, IX, VIII

Recite[234] psalm CV, versicles I, XVI, XIII, XX, XXX, XVII, XXXV

---

227 Fol.16r.

228 Judging by the format of the following psalm instructions on the planetary hours, it is possible that some of these numerals may be intended to indicate versicles within a given psalm and not a full psalm. However, it is impossible to determine this with certainty.

229 Fol.16v.

230 Fol.17r.

231 Uncertain numbering.

232 Fol.17v.

233 Fol.18r.

234 Fol.18v.

Recite[235] psalm CV, versicles I, VII

Prayer: Give to us, Moon, buried treasures to lie down upon.
Response: Give us your AREPO.[236]

Hour[237] of Mars

Recite psalm XV, versicles I, VII, XII, XX, XV, XX, IV
Recite[238] psalm XV, versicles I, VII, XII, XV, XXX, XIX
Recite[239] psalm XV, versicles I, VII

Prayer: Give to us, Mars, the power of Moses and the art of uncovering treasures.
Response: Which Locifuge holds.

---

235 Fol.19r.

236 Probably derived from the SATOR square formula; 'progenitor', in the preceding prayer to the Sun, is the literal translation of *Sator* in the text. Likewise, 'holds', in the prayer to Mars, translates *Tenet*, Mercury's 'skill' is *opera*, and 'revolutions', in the prayer to Jupiter, is a somewhat forced translation of *ROTaS*. AREPO is the only element of the formula that does not correspond to an actual word in the Latin lexicon.

237 Fol.20r.

238 Fol.20v.

239 Fol.21r.

Hour[240] of Mercury

Recite psalm XV, <versicles> XX, I, VII

Prayer: Allow us, Mercury, to uncover the inaccessible treasure we need.

Response: By your great skill.

Hour[241] of Jupiter

Recite psalm XV, versicles I, VII, X, V, XX, IX, VI

Recite[242] psalm XV, <versicles> XXII, I, VII, X, V, XX, IX, VI

Recite[243] psalm XX, versicles I, VII, X, V, XX, IX, VI

Recite[244] psalm X, versicles I, VII, X, V, XX, IX, VI

Recite[245] psalm V, versicles I, VII

Prayer: Allow us, we beg you Jupiter, to have wealth and a household to lead.

Response: To know his <revolutions>.

---

240 Fol.22r.
241 Fol.23r.
242 Fol.23v.
243 Fol.24r.
244 Fol.24v.
245 Fol.25r.

Hour[246] of Venus

Recite psalm C, versicles I, VII, XXV, XXX, VII, X, IX

Recite[247] psalm V, versicles I, VII, XXV, XXX, VII, X, IX

Recite[248] psalm CV, versicles I, VII, XXV, XXX, VII, X, IX

Hour[249] of Saturn

Recite psalm XC, versicles I, VII, XXV, XXX, VII, X, IX

Recite[250] psalm CX, versicles I, VII, XXV, XXX, VII, X, IX

Recite[251] psalm CXV, versicles I, VII, XXV, XXX, VII, X, IX

Recite[252] psalm XCV, versicles I, VII, XXV, XXX, VII, X, IX

Taking[253] a <piece of the host> and {...} one shall say the words of consecration and cry out:

Burst forth, buried treasure, in its own proper form, and come be taken as our first fruits <offering>.

---

246 Fol.26r.
247 Fol.26v.
248 Fol.27r.
249 Fol.28r.
250 Fol.28v.
251 Fol.29r.
252 Fol.30r.
253 Fol.31r.

KRAZVK

Krazvk

krasvk

Then one will stow the riches, receive the host, and hasten away, reciting the psalm {...}[254] and {I shall conquer ...} and you shall be fortunate.

No work shall be false or contrary to this upon which my name is written, which here I have signed and rubricated in my own script.

Cyprianus Magus Primus

The End

---

[254] Fol.31v.

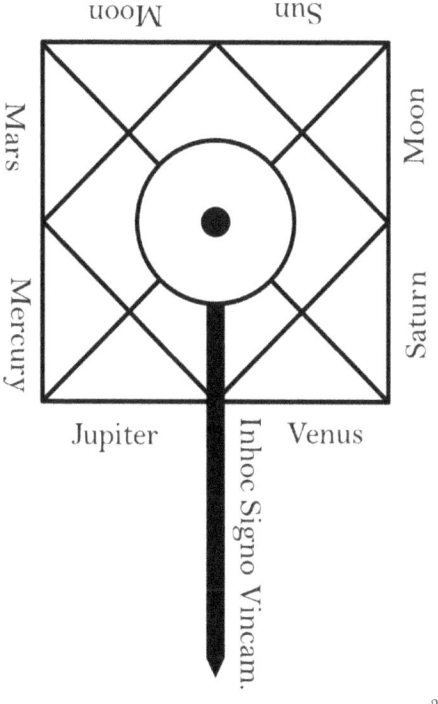

Note:

<Either> there will be a treasure, the head of the blackbird entering <its> dwelling <either forwards or backwards or one then the other>, or else there will not or there never was.

---

255 Fol.32r.
256 Fol.33r.

APPENDIX

FOLLOWING ARE THE various psalms prescribed in the *Cypriani Magici Septem Horae Magicae* for recitation during the planetary hours. These are given here for academic and interpretative purposes, as the original text proposes the consecration of a Bible, and likely, in the ritual context described, the psalms are meant to be recited from that specific book.

It should be further noted that there are some doubts regarding the psalms which are to be read during the hour of the Sun. Should the text be accurate in this regard, this is the hour with the greatest number of prescribed psalms, twenty-five, with the next greater number being four, for both Jupiter and Saturn.

The following psalms were sourced from the *Sixto-Clementine Vulgate*.[257]

---

257 Douay-Rheims + Latin Vulgate: Book of Psalms.

Psalm I

1 Beatus vir qui non abiit in consilio impiorum, et in via peccatorum non stetit, et in cathedra pestilentiæ non sedit;
2 sed in lege Domini voluntas ejus, et in lege ejus meditabitur die ac nocte.
3 Et erit tamquam lignum quod plantatum est secus decursus aquarum, quod fructum suum dabit in tempore suo: et folium ejus non defluet; et omnia quæcumque faciet prosperabuntur.
4 Non sic impii, non sic; sed tamquam pulvis quem projicit ventus a facie terræ.
5 Ideo non resurgent impii in judicio, neque peccatores in concilio justorum:
6 quoniam novit Dominus viam justorum, et iter impiorum peribit.

Psalm II

1 Quare fremuerunt gentes, et populi meditati sunt inania?
2 Astiterunt reges terræ, et principes convenerunt in unum adversus Dominum, et adversus christum ejus.
3 Dirumpamus vincula eorum, et projiciamus a nobis jugum ipsorum.
4 Qui habitat in cælis irridebit eos, et Dominus subsannabit eos.
5 Tunc loquetur ad eos in ira sua, et in furore suo conturbabit eos.
6 Ego autem constitutus sum rex ab eo super Sion, montem sanctum ejus, prædicans præceptum ejus.
7 Dominus dixit ad me: Filius meus es tu; ego hodie genui te.
8 Postula a me, et dabo tibi gentes hæreditatem tuam, et possessionem tuam terminos terræ.

9 Reges eos in virga ferrea, et tamquam vas figuli confringes eos.
10 Et nunc, reges, intelligite; erudimini, qui judicatis terram.
11 Servite Domino in timore, et exsultate ei cum tremore.
12 Apprehendite disciplinam, nequando irascatur Dominus, et pereatis de via justa.
13 Cum exarserit in brevi ira ejus, beati omnes qui confidunt in eo.

Psalm III

1 Psalmus David, cum fugeret a facie Absalom filii sui.
2 Domine, quid multiplicati sunt qui tribulant me? Multi insurgunt adversum me;
3 multi dicunt animæ meæ: Non est salus ipsi in Deo ejus.
4 Tu autem Domine, susceptor meus es, gloria mea, et exaltans caput meum.
5 Voce mea ad Dominum clamavi; et exaudivit me de monte sancto suo.
6 Ego dormivi, et soporatus sum; et exsurrexi, quia Dominus suscepit me.
7 Non timebo millia populi circumdantis me. Exsurge, Domine; salvum me fac, Deus meus.
8 Quoniam tu percussisti omnes adversantes mihi sine causa; dentes peccatorum contrivisti.
9 Domini est salus; et super populum tuum benedictio tua.

Psalm IV

1 In finem, in carminibus. Psalmus David.
2 Cum invocarem exaudivit me Deus justitiæ meæ, in tribulatione dilatasti mihi. Miserere mei, et exaudi orationem meam.

3 Filii hominum, usquequo gravi corde? ut quid diligitis vanitatem, et quæritis mendacium?
4 Et scitote quoniam mirificavit Dominus sanctum suum; Dominus exaudiet me cum clamavero ad eum.
5 Irascimini, et nolite peccare; quæ dicitis in cordibus vestris, in cubilibus vestris compungimini.
6 Sacrificate sacrificium justitiæ, et sperate in Domino. Multi dicunt: Quis ostendit nobis bona?
7 Signatum est super nos lumen vultus tui, Domine: dedisti lætitiam in corde meo.
8 A fructu frumenti, vini, et olei sui, multiplicati sunt.
9 In pace in idipsum dormiam, et requiescam;
10 quoniam tu, Domine, singulariter in spe constituisti me.

Psalm V

1 In finem, pro ea quæ hæreditatem consequitur. Psalmus David.
2 Verba mea auribus percipe, Domine; intellige clamorem meum.
3 Intende voci orationis meæ, rex meus et Deus meus.
4 Quoniam ad te orabo, Domine: mane exaudies vocem meam.
5 Mane astabo tibi, et videbo quoniam non Deus volens iniquitatem tu es.
6 Neque habitabit juxta te malignus, neque permanebunt injusti ante oculos tuos.
7 Odisti omnes qui operantur iniquitatem; perdes omnes qui loquuntur mendacium. Virum sanguinum et dolosum abominabitur Dominus.
8 Ego autem in multitudine misericordiæ tuæ introibo in domum tuam; adorabo ad templum sanctum tuum in timore tuo.

9 Domine, deduc me in justitia tua: propter inimicos meos dirige in conspectu tuo viam meam.
10 Quoniam non est in ore eorum veritas; cor eorum vanum est.
11 Sepulchrum patens est guttur eorum; linguis suis dolose agebant: judica illos, Deus. Decidant a cogitationibus suis; secundum multitudinem impietatum eorum expelle eos, quoniam irritaverunt te, Domine.
12 Et lætentur omnes qui sperant in te; in æternum exsultabunt, et habitabis in eis. Et gloriabuntur in te omnes qui diligunt nomen tuum,
13 quoniam tu benedices justo. Domine, ut scuto bonæ voluntatis tuæ coronasti nos.

Psalms VI

1 In finem, in carminibus. Psalmus David. Pro octava.
2 Domine, ne in furore tuo arguas me, neque in ira tua corripias me.
3 Miserere mei, Domine, quoniam infirmus sum; sana me, Domine, quoniam conturbata sunt ossa mea.
4 Et anima mea turbata est valde; sed tu, Domine, usquequo?
5 Convertere, Domine, et eripe animam meam; salvum me fac propter misericordiam tuam.
6 Quoniam non est in morte qui memor sit tui; in inferno autem quis confitebitur tibi?
7 Laboravi in gemitu meo; lavabo per singulas noctes lectum meum: lacrimis meis stratum meum rigabo.
8 Turbatus est a furore oculus meus; inveteravi inter omnes inimicos meos.
9 Discedite a me omnes qui operamini iniquitatem, quoniam exaudivit Dominus vocem fletus mei.

10 Exaudivit Dominus deprecationem meam; Dominus orationem meam suscepit.
11 Erubescant, et conturbentur vehementer, omnes inimici mei; convertantur, et erubescant valde velociter.

Psalm VII

1 Psalmus David, quem cantavit Domino pro verbis Chusi, filii Jemini.
2 Domine Deus meus, in te speravi; salvum me fac ex omnibus persequentibus me, et libera me:
3 nequando rapiat ut leo animam meam, dum non est qui redimat, neque qui salvum faciat.
4 Domine Deus meus, si feci istud, si est iniquitas in manibus meis,
5 si reddidi retribuentibus mihi mala, decidam merito ab inimicis meis inanis.
6 Persequatur inimicus animam meam, et comprehendat; et conculcet in terra vitam meam, et gloriam meam in pulverem deducat.
7 Exsurge, Domine, in ira tua, et exaltare in finibus inimicorum meorum: et exsurge, Domine Deus meus, in præcepto quod mandasti,
8 et synagoga populorum circumdabit te: et propter hanc in altum regredere:
9 Dominus judicat populos. Judica me, Domine, secundum justitiam meam, et secundum innocentiam meam super me.
10 Consumetur nequitia peccatorum, et diriges justum, scrutans corda et renes, Deus.
11 Justum adjutorium meum a Domino, qui salvos facit rectos corde.

12 Deus judex justus, fortis, et patiens; numquid irascitur per singulos dies?
13 Nisi conversi fueritis, gladium suum vibrabit; arcum suum tetendit, et paravit illum.
14 Et in eo paravit vasa mortis, sagittas suas ardentibus effecit.
15 Ecce parturiit injustitiam; concepit dolorem, et peperit iniquitatem.
16 Lacum aperuit, et effodit eum; et incidit in foveam quam fecit.
17 Convertetur dolor ejus in caput ejus, et in verticem ipsius iniquitas ejus descendet.
18 Confitebor Domino secundum justitiam ejus, et psallam nomini Domini altissimi.

Psalm IX

1 In finem, pro occultis filii. Psalmus David.
2 Confitebor tibi, Domine, in toto corde meo; narrabo omnia mirabilia tua.
3 Lætabor et exsultabo in te; psallam nomini tuo, Altissime.
4 In convertendo inimicum meum retrorsum; infirmabuntur, et peribunt a facie tua.
5 Quoniam fecisti judicium meum et causam meam; sedisti super thronum, qui judicas justitiam.
6 Increpasti gentes, et periit impius: nomen eorum delesti in æternum, et in sæculum sæculi.
7 Inimici defecerunt frameæ in finem, et civitates eorum destruxisti. Periit memoria eorum cum sonitu;
8 et Dominus in æternum permanet. Paravit in judicio thronum suum,
9 et ipse judicabit orbem terræ in æquitate: judicabit populos in justitia.

Appendix

10 Et factus est Dominus refugium pauperi; adjutor in opportunitatibus, in tribulatione.
11 Et sperent in te qui noverunt nomen tuum, quoniam non dereliquisti quærentes te, Domine.
12 Psallite Domino qui habitat in Sion; annuntiate inter gentes studia ejus:
13 quoniam requirens sanguinem eorum recordatus est; non est oblitus clamorem pauperum.
14 Miserere mei, Domine: vide humilitatem meam de inimicis meis,
15 qui exaltas me de portis mortis, ut annuntiem omnes laudationes tuas in portis filiæ Sion:
16 exultabo in salutari tuo. Infixæ sunt gentes in interitu quem fecerunt; in laqueo isto quem absconderunt comprehensus est pes eorum.
17 Cognoscetur Dominus judicia faciens; in operibus manuum suarum comprehensus est peccator.
18 Convertantur peccatores in infernum, omnes gentes quæ obliviscuntur Deum.
19 Quoniam non in finem oblivio erit pauperis; patientia pauperum non peribit in finem.
20 Exsurge, Domine; non confortetur homo: judicentur gentes in conspectu tuo.
21 Constitue, Domine, legislatorem super eos, ut sciant gentes quoniam homines sunt.
22 Ut quid, Domine, recessisti longe; despicis in opportunitatibus, in tribulatione?
23 Dum superbit impius, incenditur pauper: comprehenduntur in consiliis quibus cogitant.
24 Quoniam laudatur peccator in desideriis animæ suæ, et iniquus benedicitur.
25 Exacerbavit Dominum peccator: secundum multitudinem iræ suæ, non quæret.

26 Non est Deus in conspectu ejus; inquinatæ sunt viæ illius in omni tempore. Auferuntur judicia tua a facie ejus; omnium inimicorum suorum dominabitur.

27 Dixit enim in corde suo: Non movebor a generatione in generationem, sine malo.

28 Cujus maledictione os plenum est, et amaritudine, et dolo; sub lingua ejus labor et dolor.

29 Sedet in insidiis cum divitibus in occultis, ut interficiat innocentem.

30 Oculi ejus in pauperem respiciunt; insidiatur in abscondito, quasi leo in spelunca sua. Insidiatur ut rapiat pauperem; rapere pauperem dum attrahit eum.

31 In laqueo suo humiliabit eum; inclinabit se, et cadet cum dominatus fuerit pauperum.

32 Dixit enim in corde suo: Oblitus est Deus; avertit faciem suam, ne videat in finem.

33 Exsurge, Domine Deus, exaltetur manus tua; ne obliviscaris pauperum.

34 Propter quid irritavit impius Deum? dixit enim in corde suo: Non requiret.

35 Vides, quoniam tu laborem et dolorem consideras, ut tradas eos in manus tuas. Tibi derelictus est pauper; orphano tu eris adjutor.

36 Contere brachium peccatoris et maligni; quæretur peccatum illius, et non invenietur.

37 Dominus regnabit in æternum, et in sæculum sæculi; peribitis, gentes, de terra illius.

38 Desiderium pauperum exaudivit Dominus; præparationem cordis eorum audivit auris tua:

39 judicare pupillo et humili, ut non apponat ultra magnificare se homo super terram.

Appendix

Psalm X

1 In finem. Psalmus David.
2 In Domino confido; quomodo dicitis animæ meæ: Transmigra in montem sicut passer?
3 Quoniam ecce peccatores intenderunt arcum; paraverunt sagittas suas in pharetra, ut sagittent in obscuro rectos corde:
4 quoniam quæ perfecisti destruxerunt; justus autem, quid fecit?
5 Dominus in templo sancto suo; Dominus in cælo sedes ejus. Oculi ejus in pauperem respiciunt; palpebræ ejus interrogant filios hominum.
6 Dominus interrogat justum et impium; qui autem diligit iniquitatem, odit animam suam.
7 Pluet super peccatores laqueos; ignis et sulphur, et spiritus procellarum, pars calicis eorum.
8 Quoniam justus Dominus, et justitias dilexit: æquitatem vidit vultus ejus.

Psalm XIII

1 In finem. Psalmus David. Dixit insipiens in corde suo: Non est Deus. Corrupti sunt, et abominabiles facti sunt in studiis suis; non est qui faciat bonum, non est usque ad unum.
2 Dominus de cælo prospexit super filios hominum, ut videat si est intelligens, aut requirens Deum.
3 Omnes declinaverunt, simul inutiles facti sunt. Non est qui faciat bonum, non est usque ad unum. Sepulchrum patens est guttur eorum; linguis suis dolose agebant. Venenum aspidum sub labiis eorum, quorum os maledictione et amaritudine plenum est; veloces pedes eorum ad effundendum sanguinem. Contritio et infelicitas in viis

eorum, et viam pacis non cognoverunt; non est timor Dei ante oculos eorum.
4 Nonne cognoscent omnes qui operantur iniquitatem, qui devorant plebem meam sicut escam panis?
5 Dominum non invocaverunt; illic trepidaverunt timore, ubi non erat timor.
6 Quoniam Dominus in generatione justa est: consilium inopis confudistis, quoniam Dominus spes ejus est.
7 Quis dabit ex Sion salutare Israël? Cum averterit Dominus captivitatem plebis suæ, exsultabit Jacob, et lætabitur Israël.

Psalm XV

1 Tituli inscriptio, ipsi David. Conserva me, Domine, quoniam speravi in te.
2 Dixi Domino: Deus meus es tu, quoniam bonorum meorum non eges.
3 Sanctis qui sunt in terra ejus, mirificavit omnes voluntates meas in eis.
4 Multiplicatæ sunt infirmitates eorum: postea acceleraverunt. Non congregabo conventicula eorum de sanguinibus, nec memor ero nominum eorum per labia mea.
5 Dominus pars hæreditatis meæ, et calicis mei: tu es qui restitues hæreditatem meam mihi.
6 Funes ceciderunt mihi in præclaris; etenim hæreditas mea præclara est mihi.
7 Benedicam Dominum qui tribuit mihi intellectum; insuper et usque ad noctem increpuerunt me renes mei.
8 Providebam Dominum in conspectu meo semper: quoniam a dextris est mihi, ne commovear.

9 Propter hoc lætatum est cor meum, et exsultavit lingua mea; insuper et caro mea requiescet in spe.
10 Quoniam non derelinques animam meam in inferno, nec dabis sanctum tuum videre corruptionem. Notas mihi fecisti vias vitæ; adimplebis me lætitia cum vultu tuo: delectationes in dextera tua usque in finem.

Psalm XVII

1 In finem. Puero Domini David, qui locutus est Domino verba cantici hujus, in die qua eripuit eum Dominus de manu omnium inimicorum ejus, et de manu Saul, et dixit:
2 Diligam te, Domine, fortitudo mea.
3 Dominus firmamentum meum, et refugium meum, et liberator meus. Deus meus adjutor meus, et sperabo in eum; protector meus, et cornu salutis meæ, et susceptor meus.
4 Laudans invocabo Dominum, et ab inimicis meis salvus ero.
5 Circumdederunt me dolores mortis, et torrentes iniquitatis conturbaverunt me.
6 Dolores inferni circumdederunt me; præoccupaverunt me laquei mortis.
7 In tribulatione mea invocavi Dominum, et ad Deum meum clamavi: et exaudivit de templo sancto suo vocem meam; et clamor meus in conspectu ejus introivit in aures ejus.
8 Commota est, et contremuit terra; fundamenta montium conturbata sunt, et commota sunt: quoniam iratus est eis.
9 Ascendit fumus in ira ejus, et ignis a facie ejus exarsit; carbones succensi sunt ab eo.
10 Inclinavit cælos, et descendit, et caligo sub pedibus ejus.

11 Et ascendit super cherubim, et volavit; volavit super pennas ventorum.
12 Et posuit tenebras latibulum suum; in circuitu ejus tabernaculum ejus, tenebrosa aqua in nubibus aëris.
13 Præ fulgore in conspectu ejus nubes transierunt; grando et carbones ignis.
14 Et intonuit de cælo Dominus, et Altissimus dedit vocem suam: grando et carbones ignis.
15 Et misit sagittas suas, et dissipavit eos; fulgura multiplicavit, et conturbavit eos.
16 Et apparuerunt fontes aquarum, et revelata sunt fundamenta orbis terrarum, ab increpatione tua, Domine, ab inspiratione spiritus iræ tuæ.
17 Misit de summo, et accepit me; et assumpsit me de aquis multis.
18 Eripuit me de inimicis meis fortissimis, et ab his qui oderunt me. Quoniam confortati sunt super me;
19 prævenerunt me in die afflictionis meæ: et factus est Dominus protector meus.
20 Et eduxit me in latitudinem; salvum me fecit, quoniam voluit me,
21 et retribuet mihi Dominus secundum justitiam meam, et secundum puritatem manuum mearum retribuet mihi:
22 quia custodivi vias Domini, nec impie gessi a Deo meo;
23 quoniam omnia judicia ejus in conspectu meo, et justitias ejus non repuli a me.
24 Et ero immaculatus cum eo; et observabo me ab iniquitate mea.
25 Et retribuet mihi Dominus secundum justitiam meam, et secundum puritatem manuum mearum in conspectu oculorum ejus.
26 Cum sancto sanctus eris, et cum viro innocente innocens eris,

27 et cum electo electus eris, et cum perverso perverteris.
28 Quoniam tu populum humilem salvum facies, et oculos superborum humiliabis.
29 Quoniam tu illuminas lucernam meam, Domine; Deus meus, illumina tenebras meas.
30 Quoniam in te eripiar a tentatione; et in Deo meo transgrediar murum.
31 Deus meus, impolluta via ejus; eloquia Domini igne examinata: protector est omnium sperantium in se.
32 Quoniam quis deus præter Dominum? aut quis deus præter Deum nostrum?
33 Deus qui præcinxit me virtute, et posuit immaculatam viam meam;
34 qui perfecit pedes meos tamquam cervorum, et super excelsa statuens me;
35 qui docet manus meas ad prælium. Et posuisti, ut arcum æreum, brachia mea,
36 et dedisti mihi protectionem salutis tuæ: et dextera tua suscepit me, et disciplina tua correxit me in finem, et disciplina tua ipsa me docebit.
37 Dilatasti gressus meos subtus me, et non sunt infirmata vestigia mea.
38 Persequar inimicos meos, et comprehendam illos; et non convertar donec deficiant.
39 Confringam illos, nec poterunt stare; cadent subtus pedes meos.
40 Et præcinxisti me virtute ad bellum, et supplantasti insurgentes in me subtus me.
41 Et inimicos meos dedisti mihi dorsum, et odientes me disperdidisti.
42 Clamaverunt, nec erat qui salvos faceret; ad Dominum, nec exaudivit eos.

43 Et comminuam eos ut pulverem ante faciem venti; ut lutum platearum delebo eos.
44 Eripies me de contradictionibus populi; constitues me in caput gentium.
45 Populus quem non cognovi servivit mihi; in auditu auris obedivit mihi.
46 Filii alieni mentiti sunt mihi, filii alieni inveterati sunt, et claudicaverunt a semitis suis.
47 Vivit Dominus, et benedictus Deus meus, et exaltetur Deus salutis meæ.
48 Deus qui das vindictas mihi, et subdis populos sub me; liberator meus de inimicis meis iracundis.
49 Et ab insurgentibus in me exaltabis me; a viro iniquo eripies me.
50 Propterea confitebor tibi in nationibus, Domine, et nomini tuo psalmum dicam;
51 magnificans salutes regis ejus, et faciens misericordiam christo suo David, et semini ejus usque in sæculum.

Psalm XIX

1 In finem. Psalmus David.
2 Exaudiat te Dominus in die tribulationis; protegat te nomen Dei Jacob.
3 Mittat tibi auxilium de sancto, et de Sion tueatur te.
4 Memor sit omnis sacrificii tui, et holocaustum tuum pingue fiat.
5 Tribuat tibi secundum cor tuum, et omne consilium tuum confirmet.
6 Lætabimur in salutari tuo; et in nomine Dei nostri magnificabimur.
7 Impleat Dominus omnes petitiones tuas; nunc cognovi quoniam salvum fecit Dominus christum suum. Exaudiet

illum de cælo sancto suo, in potentatibus salus dexteræ ejus.
8 Hi in curribus, et hi in equis; nos autem in nomine Domini Dei nostri invocabimus.
9 Ipsi obligati sunt, et ceciderunt; nos autem surreximus, et erecti sumus.
10 Domine, salvum fac regem, et exaudi nos in die qua invocaverimus te.

Psalm XX

1 In finem. Psalmus David.
2 Domine, in virtute tua lætabitur rex, et super salutare tuum exsultabit vehementer.
3 Desiderium cordis ejus tribuisti ei, et voluntate labiorum ejus non fraudasti eum.
4 Quoniam prævenisti eum in benedictionibus dulcedinis; posuisti in capite ejus coronam de lapide pretioso.
5 Vitam petiit a te, et tribuisti ei longitudinem dierum, in sæculum, et in sæculum sæculi.
6 Magna est gloria ejus in salutari tuo; gloriam et magnum decorem impones super eum.
7 Quoniam dabis eum in benedictionem in sæculum sæculi; lætificabis eum in gaudio cum vultu tuo.
8 Quoniam rex sperat in Domino, et in misericordia Altissimi non commovebitur.
9 Inveniatur manus tua omnibus inimicis tuis; dextera tua inveniat omnes qui te oderunt.
10 Pones eos ut clibanum ignis in tempore vultus tui: Dominus in ira sua conturbabit eos, et devorabit eos ignis.
11 Fructum eorum de terra perdes, et semen eorum a filiis hominum,

12 quoniam declinaverunt in te mala; cogitaverunt consilia quæ non potuerunt stabilire.
13 Quoniam pones eos dorsum; in reliquiis tuis præparabis vultum eorum.
14 Exaltare, Domine, in virtute tua; cantabimus et psallemus virtutes tuas.

Psalm XXI

1 In finem, pro susceptione matutina. Psalmus David.
2 Deus, Deus meus, respice in me: quare me dereliquisti? longe a salute mea verba delictorum meorum.
3 Deus meus, clamabo per diem, et non exaudies; et nocte, et non ad insipientiam mihi.
4 Tu autem in sancto habitas, laus Israël.
5 In te speraverunt patres nostri; speraverunt, et liberasti eos.
6 Ad te clamaverunt, et salvi facti sunt; in te speraverunt, et non sunt confusi.
7 Ego autem sum vermis, et non homo; opprobrium hominum, et abjectio plebis.
8 Omnes videntes me deriserunt me; locuti sunt labiis, et moverunt caput.
9 Speravit in Domino, eripiat eum: salvum faciat eum, quoniam vult eum.
10 Quoniam tu es qui extraxisti me de ventre, spes mea ab uberibus matris meæ.
11 In te projectus sum ex utero; de ventre matris meæ Deus meus es tu:
12 ne discesseris a me, quoniam tribulatio proxima est, quoniam non est qui adjuvet.
13 Circumdederunt me vituli multi; tauri pingues obsederunt me.

14 Aperuerunt super me os suum, sicut leo rapiens et rugiens.
15 Sicut aqua effusus sum, et dispersa sunt omnia ossa mea: factum est cor meum tamquam cera liquescens in medio ventris mei.
16 Aruit tamquam testa virtus mea, et lingua mea adhæsit faucibus meis: et in pulverem mortis deduxisti me.
17 Quoniam circumdederunt me canes multi; concilium malignantium obsedit me. Foderunt manus meas et pedes meos;
18 dinumeraverunt omnia ossa mea. Ipsi vero consideraverunt et inspexerunt me.
19 Diviserunt sibi vestimenta mea, et super vestem meam miserunt sortem.
20 Tu autem, Domine, ne elongaveris auxilium tuum a me; ad defensionem meam conspice.
21 Erue a framea, Deus, animam meam, et de manu canis unicam meam.
22 Salva me ex ore leonis, et a cornibus unicornium humilitatem meam.
23 Narrabo nomen tuum fratribus meis; in medio ecclesiæ laudabo te.
24 Qui timetis Dominum, laudate eum; universum semen Jacob, glorificate eum.
25 Timeat eum omne semen Israël, quoniam non sprevit, neque despexit deprecationem pauperis, nec avertit faciem suam a me: et cum clamarem ad eum, exaudivit me.
26 Apud te laus mea in ecclesia magna; vota mea reddam in conspectu timentium eum.
27 Edent pauperes, et saturabuntur, et laudabunt Dominum qui requirunt eum: vivent corda eorum in sæculum sæculi.

28 Reminiscentur et convertentur ad Dominum universi fines terræ; et adorabunt in conspectu ejus universæ familiæ gentium:
29 quoniam Domini est regnum, et ipse dominabitur gentium.
30 Manducaverunt et adoraverunt omnes pingues terræ; in conspectu ejus cadent omnes qui descendunt in terram.
31 Et anima mea illi vivet; et semen meum serviet ipsi.
32 Annuntiabitur Domino generatio ventura; et annuntiabunt cæli justitiam ejus populo qui nascetur, quem fecit Dominus.

Psalm XXVI

1 Psalmus David, priusquam liniretur. Dominus illuminatio mea et salus mea: quem timebo? Dominus protector vitæ meæ: a quo trepidabo?
2 Dum appropiant super me nocentes ut edant carnes meas, qui tribulant me inimici mei, ipsi infirmati sunt et ceciderunt.
3 Si consistant adversum me castra, non timebit cor meum; si exsurgat adversum me prælium, in hoc ego sperabo.
4 Unam petii a Domino, hanc requiram, ut inhabitem in domo Domini omnibus diebus vitæ meæ; ut videam voluptatem Domini, et visitem templum ejus.
5 Quoniam abscondit me in tabernaculo suo; in die malorum protexit me in abscôndito tabernaculi sui.
6 In petra exaltavit me, et nunc exaltavit caput meum super inimicos meos. Circuivi, et immolavi in tabernaculo ejus hostiam vociferationis; cantabo, et psalmum dicam Domino.
7 Exaudi, Domine, vocem meam, qua clamavi ad te; miserere mei, et exaudi me.

8 Tibi dixit cor meum: Exquisivit te facies mea; faciem tuam, Domine, requiram.
9 Ne avertas faciem tuam a me; ne declines in ira a servo tuo. Adjutor meus esto; ne derelinquas me, neque despicias me, Deus salutaris meus.
10 Quoniam pater meus et mater mea dereliquerunt me; Dominus autem assumpsit me.
11 Legem pone mihi, Domine, in via tua, et dirige me in semitam rectam, propter inimicos meos.
12 Ne tradideris me in animas tribulantium me, quoniam insurrexerunt in me testes iniqui, et mentita est iniquitas sibi.
13 Credo videre bona Domini in terra viventium.
14 Expecta Dominum, viriliter age: et confortetur cor tuum, et sustine Dominum.

Psalm XXVII

1 Psalmus ipsi David. Ad te, Domine, clamabo; Deus meus, ne sileas a me: nequando taceas a me, et assimilabor descendentibus in lacum.
2 Exaudi, Domine, vocem deprecationis meæ dum oro ad te; dum extollo manus meas ad templum sanctum tuum.
3 Ne simul trahas me cum peccatoribus, et cum operantibus iniquitatem ne perdas me; qui loquuntur pacem cum proximo suo, mala autem in cordibus eorum.
4 Da illis secundum opera eorum, et secundum nequitiam adinventionum ipsorum. Secundum opera manuum eorum tribue illis; redde retributionem eorum ipsis.
5 Quoniam non intellexerunt opera Domini, et in opera manuum ejus destrues illos, et non ædificabis eos.
6 Benedictus Dominus, quoniam exaudivit vocem deprecationis meæ.

7 Dominus adjutor meus et protector meus; in ipso speravit cor meum, et adjutus sum: et refloruit caro mea, et ex voluntate mea confitebor ei.
8 Dominus fortitudo plebis suæ, et protector salvationum christi sui est.
9 Salvum fac populum tuum, Domine, et benedic hæreditati tuæ; et rege eos, et extolle illos usque in æternum.

Psalm XXX

1 In finem. Psalmus David, pro extasi.
2 In te, Domine, speravi; non confundar in æternum: in justitia tua libera me.
3 Inclina ad me aurem tuam; accelera ut eruas me. Esto mihi in Deum protectorem, et in domum refugii, ut salvum me facias:
4 quoniam fortitudo mea et refugium meum es tu; et propter nomen tuum deduces me et enutries me.
5 Educes me de laqueo hoc quem absconderunt mihi, quoniam tu es protector meus.
6 In manus tuas commendo spiritum meum; redemisti me, Domine Deus veritatis.
7 Odisti observantes vanitates supervacue; ego autem in Domino speravi.
8 Exsultabo, et lætabor in misericordia tua, quoniam respexisti humilitatem meam; salvasti de necessitatibus animam meam.
9 Nec conclusisti me in manibus inimici: statuisti in loco spatioso pedes meos.
10 Miserere mei, Domine, quoniam tribulor; conturbatus est in ira oculus meus, anima mea, et venter meus.

Appendix

11 Quoniam defecit in dolore vita mea, et anni mei in gemitibus. Infirmata est in paupertate virtus mea, et ossa mea conturbata sunt.

12 Super omnes inimicos meos factus sum opprobrium, et vicinis meis valde, et timor notis meis; qui videbant me foras fugerunt a me.

13 Oblivioni datus sum, tamquam mortuus a corde; factus sum tamquam vas perditum:

14 quoniam audivi vituperationem multorum commorantium in circuitu. In eo dum convenirent simul adversum me, accipere animam meam consiliati sunt.

15 Ego autem in te speravi, Domine; dixi: Deus meus es tu;

16 in manibus tuis sortes meæ: eripe me de manu inimicorum meorum, et a persequentibus me.

17 Illustra faciem tuam super servum tuum; salvum me fac in misericordia tua.

18 Domine, non confundar, quoniam invocavi te. Erubescant impii, et deducantur in infernum;

19 muta fiant labia dolosa, quæ loquuntur adversus justum iniquitatem, in superbia, et in abusione.

20 Quam magna multitudo dulcedinis tuæ, Domine, quam abscondisti timentibus te; perfecisti eis qui sperant in te in conspectu filiorum hominum!

21 Abscondes eos in abscondito faciei tuæ a conturbatione hominum; proteges eos in tabernaculo tuo, a contradictione linguarum.

22 Benedictus Dominus, quoniam mirificavit misericordiam suam mihi in civitate munita.

23 Ego autem dixi in excessu mentis meæ: Projectus sum a facie oculorum tuorum: ideo exaudisti vocem orationis meæ, dum clamarem ad te.

24 Diligite Dominum, omnes sancti ejus, quoniam veritatem requiret Dominus, et retribuet abundanter facientibus superbiam.
25 Viriliter agite, et confortetur cor vestrum, omnes qui speratis in Domino.

Psalm LV

1 In finem, pro populo qui a sanctis longe factus est. David in tituli inscriptionem, cum tenuerunt eum Allophyli in Geth.
2 Miserere mei, Deus, quoniam conculcavit me homo; tota die impugnans, tribulavit me.
3 Conculcaverunt me inimici mei tota die, quoniam multi bellantes adversum me.
4 Ab altitudine diei timebo: ego vero in te sperabo.
5 In Deo laudabo sermones meos; in Deo speravi: non timebo quid faciat mihi caro.
6 Tota die verba mea execrabantur; adversum me omnes cogitationes eorum in malum.
7 Inhabitabunt, et abscondent; ipsi calcaneum meum observabunt. Sicut sustinuerunt animam meam,
8 pro nihilo salvos facies illos; in ira populos confringes.
9 Deus, vitam meam annuntiavi tibi; posuisti lacrimas meas in conspectu tuo, sicut et in promissione tua:
10 tunc convertentur inimici mei retrorsum. In quacumque die invocavero te, ecce cognovi quoniam Deus meus es.
11 In Deo laudabo verbum; in Domino laudabo sermonem. In Deo speravi: non timebo quid faciat mihi homo.
12 In me sunt, Deus, vota tua, quæ reddam, laudationes tibi:
13 quoniam eripuisti animam meam de morte, et pedes meos de lapsu, ut placeam coram Deo in lumine viventium.

Psalm LX
1 In finem. In hymnis David.
2 Exaudi, Deus, deprecationem meam; intende orationi meæ.
3 A finibus terræ ad te clamavi, dum anxiaretur cor meum; in petra exaltasti me. Deduxisti me,
4 quia factus es spes mea: turris fortitudinis a facie inimici.
5 Inhabitabo in tabernaculo tuo in sæcula; protegar in velamento alarum tuarum.
6 Quoniam tu, Deus meus, exaudisti orationem meam; dedisti hæreditatem timentibus nomen tuum.
7 Dies super dies regis adjicies; annos ejus usque in diem generationis et generationis.
8 Permanet in æternum in conspectu Dei: misericordiam et veritatem ejus quis requiret?
9 Sic psalmum dicam nomini tuo in sæculum sæculi, ut reddam vota mea de die in diem.

Psalm LXII
1 Psalmus David, cum esset in deserto Idumææ.
2 Deus, Deus meus, ad te de luce vigilo. Sitivit in te anima mea; quam multipliciter tibi caro mea!
3 In terra deserta, et invia, et inaquosa, sic in sancto apparui tibi, ut viderem virtutem tuam et gloriam tuam.
4 Quoniam melior est misericordia tua super vitas, labia mea laudabunt te.
5 Sic benedicam te in vita mea, et in nomine tuo levabo manus meas.
6 Sicut adipe et pinguedine repleatur anima mea, et labiis exsultationis laudabit os meum.
7 Si memor fui tui super stratum meum, in matutinis meditabor in te.

8 Quia fuisti adjutor meus, et in velamento alarum tuarum exsultabo.
9 Adhæsit anima mea post te; me suscepit dextera tua.
10 Ipsi vero in vanum quæsierunt animam meam: introibunt in inferiora terræ;
11 tradentur in manus gladii: partes vulpium erunt.
12 Rex vero lætabitur in Deo; laudabuntur omnes qui jurant in eo: quia obstructum est os loquentium iniqua.

Psalm LXV

1 In finem. Canticum psalmi resurrectionis. Jubilate Deo, omnis terra;
2 psalmum dicite nomini ejus; date gloriam laudi ejus.
3 Dicite Deo: Quam terribilia sunt opera tua, Domine! in multitudine virtutis tuæ mentientur tibi inimici tui.
4 Omnis terra adoret te, et psallat tibi; psalmum dicat nomini tuo.
5 Venite, et videte opera Dei: terribilis in consiliis super filios hominum.
6 Qui convertit mare in aridam; in flumine pertransibunt pede: ibi lætabimur in ipso.
7 Qui dominatur in virtute sua in æternum; oculi ejus super gentes respiciunt: qui exasperant non exaltentur in semetipsis.
8 Benedicite, gentes, Deum nostrum, et auditam facite vocem laudis ejus:
9 qui posuit animam meam ad vitam, et non dedit in commotionem pedes meos.
10 Quoniam probasti nos, Deus; igne nos examinasti, sicut examinatur argentum.

Appendix

11 Induxisti nos in laqueum; posuisti tribulationes in dorso nostro;
12 imposuisti homines super capita nostra. Transivimus per ignem et aquam, et eduxisti nos in refrigerium.
13 Introibo in domum tuam in holocaustis; reddam tibi vota mea
14 quæ distinxerunt labia mea: et locutum est os meum in tribulatione mea.
15 Holocausta medullata offeram tibi, cum incenso arietum; offeram tibi boves cum hircis.
16 Venite, audite, et narrabo, omnes qui timetis Deum, quanta fecit animæ meæ.
17 Ad ipsum ore meo clamavi, et exaltavi sub lingua mea.
18 Iniquitatem si aspexi in corde meo, non exaudiet Dominus.
19 Propterea exaudivit Deus, et attendit voci deprecationis meæ.
20 Benedictus Deus, qui non amovit orationem meam, et misericordiam suam a me.

Psalm LXIX

1 In finem. Psalmus David in rememorationem, quod salvum fecerit eum Dominus.
2 Deus, in adjutorium meum intende; Domine, ad adjuvandum me festina.
3 Confundantur, et revereantur, qui quærunt animam meam.
4 Avertantur retrorsum, et erubescant, qui volunt mihi mala; avertantur statim erubescentes qui dicunt mihi: Euge, euge!

5 Exsultent et lætentur in te omnes qui quærunt te; et dicant semper: Magnificetur Dominus, qui diligunt salutare tuum.
6 Ego vero egenus et pauper sum; Deus, adjuva me. Adjutor meus et liberator meus es tu; Domine, ne moreris.

Psalm XC

1 Laus cantici David. Qui habitat in adjutorio Altissimi, in protectione Dei cæli commorabitur.
2 Dicet Domino: Susceptor meus es tu, et refugium meum; Deus meus, sperabo in eum.
3 Quoniam ipse liberavit me de laqueo venantium, et a verbo aspero.
4 Scapulis suis obumbrabit tibi, et sub pennis ejus sperabis.
5 Scuto circumdabit te veritas ejus: non timebis a timore nocturno;
6 a sagitta volante in die, a negotio perambulante in tenebris, ab incursu, et dæmonio meridiano.
7 Cadent a latere tuo mille, et decem millia a dextris tuis; ad te autem non appropinquabit.
8 Verumtamen oculis tuis considerabis, et retributionem peccatorum videbis.
9 Quoniam tu es, Domine, spes mea; Altissimum posuisti refugium tuum.
10 Non accedet ad te malum, et flagellum non appropinquabit tabernaculo tuo.
11 Quoniam angelis suis mandavit de te, ut custodiant te in omnibus viis tuis.
12 In manibus portabunt te, ne forte offendas ad lapidem pedem tuum.
13 Super aspidem et basiliscum ambulabis, et conculcabis leonem et draconem.

14 Quoniam in me speravit, liberabo eum; protegam eum, quoniam cognovit nomen meum.
15 Clamabit ad me, et ego exaudiam eum; cum ipso sum in tribulatione: eripiam eum, et glorificabo eum.
16 Longitudine dierum replebo eum, et ostendam illi salutare meum.

Psalm XCV

1 Canticum ipsi David, quando domus ædificabatur post captivitatem. Cantate Domino canticum novum; cantate Domino omnis terra.
2 Cantate Domino, et benedicite nomini ejus; annuntiate de die in diem salutare ejus.
3 Annuntiate inter gentes gloriam ejus; in omnibus populis mirabilia ejus.
4 Quoniam magnus Dominus, et laudabilis nimis: terribilis est super omnes deos.
5 Quoniam omnes dii gentium dæmonia; Dominus autem cælos fecit.
6 Confessio et pulchritudo in conspectu ejus; sanctimonia et magnificentia in sanctificatione ejus.
7 Afferte Domino, patriæ gentium, afferte Domino gloriam et honorem;
8 afferte Domino gloriam nomini ejus. Tollite hostias, et introite in atria ejus;
9 adorate Dominum in atrio sancto ejus. Commoveatur a facie ejus universa terra;
10 dicite in gentibus, quia Dominus regnavit. Etenim correxit orbem terræ, qui non commovebitur; judicabit populos in æquitate.
11 Lætentur cæli, et exsultet terra; commoveatur mare et plenitudo ejus;

12 gaudebunt campi, et omnia quæ in eis sunt. Tunc exsultabunt omnia ligna silvarum
13 a facie Domini, quia venit, quoniam venit judicare terram. Judicabit orbem terræ in æquitate, et populos in veritate sua.

Psalm C

1 Psalmus ipsi David. Misericordiam et judicium cantabo tibi, Domine; psallam,
2 et intelligam in via immaculata: quando venies ad me? Perambulabam in innocentia cordis mei, in medio domus meæ.
3 Non proponebam ante oculos meos rem injustam; facientes prævaricationes odivi; non adhæsit mihi
4 cor pravum; declinantem a me malignum non cognoscebam.
5 Detrahentem secreto proximo suo, hunc persequebar: superbo oculo, et insatiabili corde, cum hoc non edebam.
6 Oculi mei ad fideles terræ, ut sedeant mecum; ambulans in via immaculata, hic mihi ministrabat.
7 Non habitabit in medio domus meæ qui facit superbiam; qui loquitur iniqua non direxit in conspectu oculorum meorum.
8 In matutino interficiebam omnes peccatores terræ, ut disperderem de civitate Domini omnes operantes iniquitatem.

Psalm CI

1 Oratio pauperis, cum anxius fuerit, et in conspectu Domini effuderit precem suam.
2 Domine, exaudi orationem meam, et clamor meus ad te veniat.
3 Non avertas faciem tuam a me: in quacumque die tribulor, inclina ad me aurem tuam; in quacumque die invocavero te, velociter exaudi me.
4 Quia defecerunt sicut fumus dies mei, et ossa mea sicut cremium aruerunt.
5 Percussus sum ut fœnum, et aruit cor meum, quia oblitus sum comedere panem meum.
6 A voce gemitus mei adhæsit os meum carni meæ.
7 Similis factus sum pellicano solitudinis; factus sum sicut nycticorax in domicilio.
8 Vigilavi, et factus sum sicut passer solitarius in tecto.
9 Tota die exprobrabant mihi inimici mei, et qui laudabant me adversum me jurabant:
10 quia cinerem tamquam panem manducabam, et potum meum cum fletu miscebam,
11 a facie iræ et indignationis tuæ: quia elevans allisisti me.
12 Dies mei sicut umbra declinaverunt, et ego sicut fœnum arui.
13 Tu autem, Domine, in æternum permanes, et memoriale tuum in generationem et generationem.
14 Tu exsurgens misereberis Sion, quia tempus miserendi ejus, quia venit tempus:
15 quoniam placuerunt servis tuis lapides ejus, et terræ ejus miserebuntur.
16 Et timebunt gentes nomen tuum, Domine, et omnes reges terræ gloriam tuam:

17 quia ædificavit Dominus Sion, et videbitur in gloria sua.
18 Respexit in orationem humilium et non sprevit precem eorum.
19 Scribantur hæc in generatione altera, et populus qui creabitur laudabit Dominum.
20 Quia prospexit de excelso sancto suo; Dominus de cælo in terram aspexit:
21 ut audiret gemitus compeditorum; ut solveret filios interemptorum:
22 ut annuntient in Sion nomen Domini, et laudem ejus in Jerusalem:
23 in conveniendo populos in unum, et reges, ut serviant Domino.
24 Respondit ei in via virtutis suæ: Paucitatem dierum meorum nuntia mihi:
25 ne revoces me in dimidio dierum meorum, in generationem et generationem anni tui.
26 Initio tu, Domine, terram fundasti, et opera manuum tuarum sunt cæli.
27 Ipsi peribunt, tu autem permanes; et omnes sicut vestimentum veterascent. Et sicut opertorium mutabis eos, et mutabuntur;
28 tu autem idem ipse es, et anni tui non deficient.
29 Filii servorum tuorum habitabunt, et semen eorum in sæculum dirigetur.

Psalm CV

1 Alleluja. Confitemini Domino, quoniam bonus, quoniam in sæculum misericordia ejus.
2 Quis loquetur potentias Domini; auditas faciet omnes laudes ejus?
3 Beati qui custodiunt judicium, et faciunt justitiam in omni

tempore.
4 Memento nostri, Domine, in beneplacito populi tui; visita nos in salutari tuo:
5 ad videndum in bonitate electorum tuorum; ad lætandum in lætitia gentis tuæ: ut lauderis cum hæreditate tua.
6 Peccavimus cum patribus nostris: injuste egimus; iniquitatem fecimus.
7 Patres nostri in Ægypto non intellexerunt mirabilia tua; non fuerunt memores multitudinis misericordiæ tuæ. Et irritaverunt ascendentes in mare, mare Rubrum;
8 et salvavit eos propter nomen suum, ut notam faceret potentiam suam.
9 Et increpuit mare Rubrum et exsiccatum est, et deduxit eos in abyssis sicut in deserto.
10 Et salvavit eos de manu odientium, et redemit eos de manu inimici.
11 Et operuit aqua tribulantes eos; unus ex eis non remansit.
12 Et crediderunt verbis ejus, et laudaverunt laudem ejus.
13 Cito fecerunt; obliti sunt operum ejus: et non sustinuerunt consilium ejus.
14 Et concupierunt concupiscentiam in deserto, et tentaverunt Deum in inaquoso.
15 Et dedit eis petitionem ipsorum, et misit saturitatem in animas eorum.
16 Et irritaverunt Moysen in castris; Aaron, sanctum Domini.
17 Aperta est terra, et deglutivit Dathan, et operuit super congregationem Abiron.
18 Et exarsit ignis in synagoga eorum: flamma combussit peccatores.
19 Et fecerunt vitulum in Horeb, et adoraverunt sculptile.
20 Et mutaverunt gloriam suam in similitudinem vituli comedentis fœnum.

21 Obliti sunt Deum qui salvavit eos; qui fecit magnalia in Ægypto,
22 mirabilia in terra Cham, terribilia in mari Rubro.
23 Et dixit ut disperderet eos, si non Moyses, electus ejus, stetisset in confractione in conspectu ejus, ut averteret iram ejus, ne disperderet eos.
24 Et pro nihilo habuerunt terram desiderabilem; non crediderunt verbo ejus.
25 Et murmuraverunt in tabernaculis suis; non exaudierunt vocem Domini.
26 Et elevavit manum suam super eos ut prosterneret eos in deserto:
27 et ut dejiceret semen eorum in nationibus, et dispergeret eos in regionibus.
28 Et initiati sunt Beelphegor, et comederunt sacrificia mortuorum.
29 Et irritaverunt eum in adinventionibus suis, et multiplicata est in eis ruina.
30 Et stetit Phinees, et placavit, et cessavit quassatio.
31 Et reputatum est ei in justitiam, in generationem et generationem usque in sempiternum.
32 Et irritaverunt eum ad aquas contradictionis, et vexatus est Moyses propter eos:
33 quia exacerbaverunt spiritum ejus, et distinxit in labiis suis.
34 Non disperdiderunt gentes quas dixit Dominus illis:
35 et commisti sunt inter gentes, et didicerunt opera eorum;
36 et servierunt sculptilibus eorum, et factum est illis in scandalum.
37 Et immolaverunt filios suos et filias suas dæmoniis.
38 Et effuderunt sanguinem innocentem, sanguinem filiorum suorum et filiarum suarum, quas sacrificaverunt sculptilibus Chanaan. Et infecta est terra in sanguinibus,

39 et contaminata est in operibus eorum: et fornicati sunt in adinventionibus suis.
40 Et iratus est furore Dominus in populum suum, et abominatus est hæreditatem suam.
41 Et tradidit eos in manus gentium; et dominati sunt eorum qui oderunt eos.
42 Et tribulaverunt eos inimici eorum, et humiliati sunt sub manibus eorum;
43 sæpe liberavit eos. Ipsi autem exacerbaverunt eum in consilio suo, et humiliati sunt in iniquitatibus suis.
44 Et vidit cum tribularentur, et audivit orationem eorum.
45 Et memor fuit testamenti sui, et pœnituit eum secundum multitudinem misericordiæ suæ:
46 et dedit eos in misericordias, in conspectu omnium qui ceperant eos.
47 Salvos nos fac, Domine Deus noster, et congrega nos de nationibus: ut confiteamur nomini sancto tuo, et gloriemur in laude tua.
48 Benedictus Dominus Deus Israël, a sæculo et usque in sæculum; et dicet omnis populus: Fiat, fiat.

Psalm CX

1 Alleluja. Confitebor tibi, Domine, in toto corde meo, in consilio justorum, et congregatione.
2 Magna opera Domini: exquisita in omnes voluntates ejus.
3 Confessio et magnificentia opus ejus, et justitia ejus manet in sæculum sæculi.
4 Memoriam fecit mirabilium suorum, misericors et miserator Dominus.
5 Escam dedit timentibus se; memor erit in sæculum testamenti sui.

6 Virtutem operum suorum annuntiabit populo suo,
7 ut det illis hæreditatem gentium. Opera manuum ejus veritas et judicium.
8 Fidelia omnia mandata ejus, confirmata in sæculum sæculi, facta in veritate et æquitate.
9 Redemptionem misit populo suo; mandavit in æternum testamentum suum. Sanctum et terribile nomen ejus.
10 Initium sapientiæ timor Domini; intellectus bonus omnibus facientibus eum: laudatio ejus manet in sæculum sæculi.

Psalm CXV

1 Alleluja. Credidi, propter quod locutus sum; ego autem humiliatus sum nimis.
2 Ego dixi in excessu meo: Omnis homo mendax.
3 Quid retribuam Domino pro omnibus quæ retribuit mihi?
4 Calicem salutaris accipiam, et nomen Domini invocabo.
5 Vota mea Domino reddam coram omni populo ejus.
6 Pretiosa in conspectu Domini mors sanctorum ejus.
7 O Domine, quia ego servus tuus; ego servus tuus, et filius ancillæ tuæ. Dirupisti vincula mea:
8 tibi sacrificabo hostiam laudis, et nomen Domini invocabo.
9 Vota mea Domino reddam in conspectu omnis populi ejus;
10 in atriis domus Domini, in medio tui, Jerusalem.

BIBLIOGRAPHY

Manuscript Sources

Archivo Castro Vicente (ACV):

ANON. - *El Verdadero Libro de San Ciprian*, n.p.: n.d.

Arquivo Nacional da Torre do Tombo (ANTT):

Tribunal do Santo Oficio, Inquisição de Coimbra, Processos, n°723, n°727, n°730, n°732, n°2065, n°3949, n°3951, n°4060, n°5197, n°5634, n°7258, n°7680, n°7689, n°7692, n°7779, n°8183, n°8628, n°9713, n°9846.

Tribunal do Santo Oficio, Inquisição de Coimbra, Promotor, Livro n°326, Livro n°378, Livro n°392, Livro n°394, Livro n°416.

Tribunal do Santo Oficio, Inquisição de Lisboa, Processos, n°2393, n°7317, n°11103.

Biblioteca Geral da Universidade de Coimbra (BGUC):

Reservados, *[Orações Vàrias para Afugentar o Demonio]*, n.d., MS. 2559.

Biblioteca Nacional de Portugal (BNP):

Manuscritos Reservados, *Cypriani Magiij Septem Horae Magicae, Editae ab ipso Bernae 154...*, MSS. 174, n. 155.

Sociedade Martins Sarmento (SMS):

Manuscritos, Série: *Citânia e Sabroso*, Caderno 37.

Printed sources

ANON. - *El Libro Infernal: Tratado Completo de las Ciencias Ocultas*, n.p.: Biblioteca Esotérica Herrou Aragón, n.d.

ANON. - *Heptameron ó Elementos Magicos Compuesto Por el Gran Cipriano Famoso Magico. Traducido el Latin y de Este al Frances por Esterhazy y Ultimamente e la Lengua Castellana, Por Fabio Salazar y Quinocees, Astrologo, Alquimista e Profundo Naturalista*. Barcelona: Parsival Ediciones, 1989.

ANON. - *Libro de San Cipriano: Libro Completo de Verdadera Magia o Sea Tesoro Del Hechicero*. Mexico: Biblioteca Ciencias Ocutas, n.d.

ANON. - *O Grande Livro de S. Cypriano: ou Thesouro do Feiticeiro*. Lisbon: Livraria Economica, n.d.

ANON. - *O Verdadeiro Livro de S. Cypriano: ou o Thesouro Particular do Feiticeiro*. Porto: Livraria Portugueza, n.d.

ANON. - *O Verdadeiro e Ultimo Livro de S. Cypriano*. Porto: Typographia de A. J. da Silva Teixeira, 1881.

SUFURINO, Jonas - *La Magia Suprema Negra, Roja e Infernal de los Caldeos y de los Egipcios*. Buenos Aires: Orden de la Sociedad Oculista Mundial, n.d.

Secondary sources

ATTRELL, Dan and PORRECA, David - 'Introduction,' in MAJRITI, Maslamah ibn Ahmad (auth.), ATTRELL, Dan and PORRECA, David (eds., trans.) - *Picatrix: A Medieval Treatise on Astral Magic*. University Park: The Pennsylvania State University Press, 2009.

BARREIRO, Bernardo - *Brujos y Astrólogos de la Inquisición de Galicia*. La Coruña: Extramuros Edición, 2010.

BASSET, René - *Les Apocryphes Ethiopiens – IV: Les Prières de S.*

BJÖRN GÅRDBÄCK, Johannes - 'Cyprianus Formaning' in CUMMINS, Alexander, HATHAWAY DIAZ, Jesse and ZAHRI, Jennifer (eds.) - *Cyprana: Old World*. Seattle: Revelore Press, 2017, pp. 36–50.

CARDAILLAC-HERMOSILLA, Yvette - 'Le Magicien-Guérisseur du Carnet de Voyage de 1835 d'Antoine d'Abbadie'. *Lapurdum: Euskal Ikerketen Aldizkaria*, 2:2 (1997), p. 93-107.

CASTRO VICENTE, Félix Fco. - 'El Libro de San Cipriano (I)'. Hibris: Revista da Bibliofilia, V:27 (2005) pp. 15-25.

CASTRO VICENTE, Félix Fco. - 'El Libro de San Cipriano (y II)'. Hibris: Revista da Bibliofilia, V:28 (2005) pp. 32-41.

CASTRO VICENTE, Félix - «San Cipriano o Mago: De Oracións, Cipriaillos e Tesouros. Santiago de Compostela: Xunta de Galicia; Consellería de Cultura, Educación e Universidade; Secretaría Xeral de Cultura; Museo Etnolóxico. Ribadavia, 2021.

COELHO, Adolfo - *Obra Etnográfica*. Lisbon: Publicações Dom Quixote, 1993, 2 vols.

COELHO, F. Adolpho - 'Notas e Paralleos Folkloricos I: Tradições Relativas a S. Cypriano. *Revista Lusitana*, I (1887-1888), pp. 166-174.

COELHO, Francisco Adolpho - *Tales of Old Lusitania: From the Folk-Lore of Portugal*. London: Swan Sonneschein & Co., 1888.

CORREIA, João da Silva - 'Adolfo Coelho'. Revista da Fauldade de Letras, I:1-2 (1993), pp. 1-10.

CUNHA, Xavier da - 'Antonio da Silva Tullio'. Occidente: *Revista Illustrada de Portugal e do Extrangeiro*, VII:183 (1884), p. 18, VII:184 (1884), p. 27, VII:185 (1884), p.

38.

DAVIES, Owen - *Grimoires: A History of Magic Books*; Oxford; New York: Oxford University Press, 2009.

DILLINGER, Johannes - *Magical Treasure Hunting in Europe and North America: A History*. New York: Palgrave Macmillan, 2012.

'Douay-Rheims + Latin Vulgate: Book of Psalms.' https://www.drbo.org/drl/chapter/21001.htm. *Douay-Rheims Bible Online, Official Catholic Version with Search*. Accessed September XX, 2025.

DUNI, Matteo - 'Esorcisti o Stregoni? Identità Professionale del Clero e Inquisizione a Modena nel Primo Cinquecento.' *Mélanges de l'École Française de Rome, Italie et Méditerranée*. 115:1 (2003), pp. 263-85.

EMERSON, Mark Cooper - 'The Devil in the Court of the King: Popular Prophecy and the Inquisition in Seventeenth-century Portugal', in LIMA, Luís Filipe Silvério and MEGIANI, Ana Paula Torres - *Visions Prophecies and Divinations: Early Modern Messianism and Millenarianism in Iberian America, Spain and Portugal*. Leiden; Boston: Brill, 2016, pp.136-158.

ESPÍRITO SANTO, Moisés - *A Religião Popular Portuguesa*. Lisbon: Assírio & Alvim, 1990, p. 125.

FORSHAW, Peter J. - 'From Occult Ekphrasis to Magical Art: Transforming Text into Talismanic Images in the Scriptorium of Alfonso X.' in KIYANRAD, Sarah, THEIS, Christoffer and WILLER, Laura - *Bild und Schrift auf 'Magischer' Artefakten*. Berlin; Boston: De Gruyter, 2018.

JOHNSON, Brian - *Necromancy in the Medici Library: An Edition and Translation of Excerpts from Biblioteca Mediceaa Laurenziana, MS Plut. 89 sup. 38*. West Yorkshire: Hadean Press, 2020.

Bibliography

LEAL, João - *Etnografias Portuguesas (1870 – 1970): Cultura Popular e Identidade Nacional*. Lisbon: Publicações Dom Quixote, 2000.

LEAL, João - 'Prefácio', in COELHO, Adolfo - *Obra Etnográfica*. Lisbon: Publicações Dom Quixote, 1993, vol. 1, pp. 13-36.

LEITÃO, José Carlos Vieira - *Learned Magic in Early Modern Portugal*. Coimbra: Faculdade de Letras da Universidade de Coimbra; Universidade de Coimbra, 2024 (PhD thesis).

LEITÃO, José - *Fairy Women from the Portuguese Book of Lineages of Count Dom Pedro: From Politics to Mysticism and Magic*. West Yorkshire: Papaveria Press, 2024.

LEITÃO, José - *Opuscula Cypriani: Variations on the Book of Saint Cyprian and Related Literature*. West Yorkshire: Hadean Press, 2019.

LEITÃO, José - 'Searching for Cyprian in Portuguese Ethnography', in CUMMINS, Alexander, HATHAWAY DIAZ, Jesse and ZAHRI, Jennifer (eds.) - *Cypriana: Old World*. Seattle: Revelore Press, 2017, pp. 117-162.

LEITÃO, José - *The Book of St. Cyprian: The Sorcerer's Treasure*. West Yorkshire: Hadean Press, 2014.

LEITÃO, José - *The Coimbra Book of Saint Cyprian: Ms. 2559 – Various Prayers to Drive Away the Devil*. West Yorkshire: Hadean Press, 2020.

LEITÃO, José - *The Immaterial Book of St. Cyprian: Folk Concepts & Views on The Book as a Cultural Item Through the Reading of Folk Narratives*. Seattle: Revelore Press, 2017.

MAGGI, Humberto - *Sujurno*. n.p.: Nephilim Press, 2017.

MORALES ESTÉVES, Roberto - 'Los Grimorios y Recetarios Mágicos: Del Mítico Salomón al Clérigo Nigromante,' in LARA, Eva and MONTANER,

Alberto (coords.) - *Señales, Portentos y Demonios: La Magia en la Literatura y la Cultura Españolas del Renacimiento.* Salamanca: Sociedad de Estudios Medievales y Renacentistas, 2004, pp. 537-554.

NA and MPP - Antonio da Silva Túlio: Carnide, 1818 – Lisboa, 1884*. TECOP: Textos e Contexto do Orientalismo Português. https://tecop.bnportugal.gov.pt/np4/file/446/Ant_nio_da_Silva_T_lio__SITE.pdf. Accessed June 7, 2024.

NORONHA, Francisco de (D.) - 'Dr. Francisco Martins de Gouveia Moraes Sarmento'. *Occidente: Revista Illustrada de Portugal e do Extrangeiro*, XXII:744 (1899), p. 190-1.

PAIVA, José Pedro - *Bruxaria e Superstição: Num País sem "Caça às Bruxas"*. Lisbon: Editorial Notícias, 2002.

PARAFITA, Alexandre - *A Mitologia dos Mouros: Lendas, Mitos, Serpentes, Tesouros.* Canelas: Edições Gailivro, 2006.

RIBEIRO, António Vitor - *O Auto dos Místicos*. Lisbon: Chiado Editora, 2015.

RISCO, Vicente - 'Los Tesoros Legendarios da Galicia'. *Revista de Dialectología y Tradiciones Populares*, 6:2 (1950), pp. 185-213, 403-429.

SAIF, Liana - *The Arabic Influences on Early Modern Occult Philosophy*. New York: Palgrave Macmillan, 2015.

SARMENTO, F. Martins - 'A Propósito dos «Roteiros de Thesouros»'. *Revista de Guimarães*, V (1888) 5-10.

SIERRA, Julio - *Procesos en la Inquisición de Toledo (1575-1610): Manuscrito de Halle*. Madrid: Editorial Trotta, 2005.

SILVA, Ana Luiza de Oliveira - *Nova Configuração da Inquisição Portuguesa em Meio a Iluminados e Iluministas: 1720-1821*. São Paulo: Universidade de São Paulo – Faculdade de Filosofia, Letras e Ciência Humanas – Departamento de História, 2009 (Master's thesis).

Bibliography

SILVA, Francisco Artur da - *Catalogo das Livrarias do Illustre Académico Antonio da Silva Tulio e do Districto advogado Augusto M. de Quintella Emauz, Ambos Já Fallecidos. Obras Classicas, Latinas, Portuguezas e Francesas, de Sciencias, Historia e Litteratura. Obras Raras e Curiosas em Todas as Classes; Importante Collecção de Obras de Jurisprudencia.* Lisbon: Typografia da Viuva Sousa Neves, 1884.

SUÁREZ LÓPEZ, Jesús - *Tesoros, Ayalgas y Chalgueiros: La Fiebre del Oro en Asturias*. Gijón: Funcación Municipal de Cultura, Educación y Universidad Popular, 2001.

SUFURINO, Jonas and SAVEDOW, Steve (trans.) - *The Supreme Black, Red and Infernal Magic of the Chaldeans and Egyptians*. West Yorkshire: Hadean Pess, 2022.

TAUSIET, María - *Urban Magic in Early Modern Spain: Abracadabra Omnipotens*. New York: Palgrave Macmillian, 2014.

VASCONCELLOS, J. Leite - *Tradiçōes Populares de Portugal*. Porto: Livraria Portuense de Clavel &C.ª, 1882.

VEIGA, Marcos Antonio Lopes - *Sob a Capa Negra: Necromancia e Feitiçaria, Curanderismo e Práticas Mágicas de Homens em Aragão (Séculos XVI e XVII)*. São Paulo: Universidade de São Paulo – Faculdade de Filosofia, Letras e Ciências Humanas; Departamento de Historia, 2011 (PhD thesis).

www.ingramcontent.com/pod-product-compliance
Lightning Source LLC
Chambersburg PA
CBHW040250170426
43191CB00018B/2363